Jo Chick M.A., D.S.A., D.S.W. has more than twenty years of experience helping families where there is a drinking problem and is recognised for her skill as a teacher of professionals and lay counsellors. In her private psychotherapy practice she has specialised in the recovery from alcoholism, depression, anxiety and stress disorders and a wide range of sexual and marital problems.

Dr Jonathan Chick MA(Cantab) MBChB M Phil FRCPE FRCPsych is Consultant Psychiatrist at the Alcohol Problems Clinic, Royal Edinburgh Hospital and a Senior Lecturer at Edinburgh University, Scotland. His practice and research in the early identification and treatment of problem drinkers has been acknowledged worldwide. He has been an advisor to the World Health Organisation, and government bodies in the USA, Canada, Australia, Brazil as well as in Britain.

Drinking Problems

JO CHICK and
DR. JONATHAN CHICK

POSITIVE HEALTH GUIDE

An OPTIMA book

Copyright © Jo Chick & Dr. Jonathan Chick 1984, 1992

The right of Jo Chick and Dr Jonathan Chick to be identified
as author of this work has been asserted by them
in accordance with the Copyright, Designs and Patents Act 1988.

First published in 1984 by
Churchill Livingstone
This revised edition published
1992 by Optima

A CIP catalogue record for this book is available
from the British Library

0 356 20371 9

Optima
a Division of
Little, Brown and Company (UK) Limited
165 Great Dover Street
London
SE1 4YA

Typeset by Leaper & Gard Ltd, Bristol, England
Printed and bound in Great Britain by
Clays Ltd, St Ives plc

Contents

Acknowledgments

We owe a great deal to numerous colleagues and friends and above all to our patients and their families for sharing their experiences with us. Thanks for the cartoons to WEEF, Peter Joyce, *Punch*, Dietmar Kainrath and Alcohol Concern.

1

Is this book for me?

We hope this book will help people with drinking problems, and those who are worried about their drinking or who have friends or relatives who complain about it. The book is intended also to be of use to the family and friends of problem drinkers. 'I'm fed-up of hearing good advice,' say some problem drinkers. They feel they have been nagged enough: 'I can't see what everyone is worried about.' Or perhaps they see there is a problem, but 'people don't realise how difficult it is for me to change my drinking – it's such an important part of my life.' Friends and relatives, too, may have been offered plenty of advice, often conflicting. Some say to them 'Never give up trying,' while others say 'It's up to him, no-one else can do anything.' Sometimes the advice is 'Stick by her, even though she's making life difficult for you all,' while elsewhere it's 'You must be hard; threaten divorce or she'll never do anything to help herself.' Sometimes the relatives are very embarrassed, they cover up for the drinker and try to keep their worries hidden. They may then feel alone and bewildered.

CAN A PROBLEM DRINKER EVER CHANGE?

Yes. The majority of people in trouble with their drinking change their pattern successfully or stop altogether. They usually find that life without alcohol, or with less, is not as bad as they feared, and that after some time it can be more enjoyable than their previous way of life. Often, people have stopped or cut down their drinking entirely on their own or just with the family's help. Others seek special help.

It is known how alcohol can sometimes cause harm, but at present we cannot say for certain why one person gets into difficulty with drinking while another does not. Nor can we definitely say who will recover completely from a drinking problem, and who is likely to continue drinking or get very ill and even die.

But however small the problems surrounding the drinking, the sooner something is done the better. Once a job is lost, or health damaged, or a marriage harmed, it is that much harder to put things right.

WHAT SORT OF BOOK IS THIS?

This is a handbook: don't feel you have to read it from beginning to end. Dip into it. If you find parts helpful, underline them or mark the page. We have tried to be brief – and that means that some of the advice may perhaps sound over-simple.

When we quote former clients or patients we are using their words with their permission, direct from letters sent to us.

We would appreciate your comments on whether the book has something in it which helped you. If you feel you have tried absolutely everything here already, and to no avail, it might be worth checking if you tried consistently – because sometimes in a crisis we try anything almost at random. It will need thought to work out what is going to be best for you. In such a little book, we cannot answer all the questions you may have, but we hope you find something that helps you. *Don't forget, the odds are in your favour if you keep on trying.*

2

What is a drinking problem?

The effects of alcohol vary from person to person. The unpleasant effects, just as the pleasant effects – relaxation, enjoyment – depend on the person as well as the setting and the atmosphere. Alcohol makes some people noisy and jovial, others quiet and sleepy.

Having a drinking problem simply means:

- That the unpleasant side to your drinking is beginning in some way to affect your life – your nerves, health, work, family or personal relationships; OR
- That you have become 'dependent' on alcohol, that is you are beginning really to need it, or it is becoming hard to take it or leave it (this is explained on pages 14–16).

You can be dependent on alcohol without having any other problems; you can also have problems, for example, in the family or at work, without being dependent.

WHAT ARE THE UNPLEASANT EFFECTS ON EMOTIONS AND PERSONAL RELATIONSHIPS?

Alcohol is a drug that depresses the brain. This is a fact, even though most of us know the brief, bright cheery feeling that

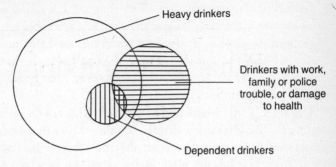

Figure 1 Not all heavy drinkers have problems. Not all drinkers with problems are dependent on alcohol.

comes with the first drink. Alcohol can actually cause severe mental depression.

Take Elaine. She had only been married a year when she suffered a miscarriage. Having been a regular drinker since 18, she turned to alcohol to dull her sense of loss. The more she drank, the more awful she felt. Yet a drink usually gave an hour or two or relaxation and release from her sadness and this was sufficient to make her continue. It was only when she stopped drinking that she realised she had recovered from her depression and was ready to go on with life. It is hard for someone who uses alcohol to dull worries and painful memories to realise it may be making them worse.

With alcohol we sometimes act very differently from normal. Although it helps us to 'let go' and this can be a good thing, for example at a party, it may also mean that the nastier side (that we all have) is more likely to come out. In some of us it brings out pettiness and jealousy towards those who are closest to us. Criticism is seen where none is intended. Drinking can make a person bad-tempered, and if alcohol brings out bottled-up envy or hate, a friendship or marriage may be threatened or destroyed.

Sometimes arguments and rows that we have had when drinking are apparently forgotten when we are sober. A very high level of alcohol in the brain prevents us from remembering what we say or do. Also, the mind tends to shut out those things we are ashamed of. However, our family and friends will remember.

Consider Tony. He is a civil servant, who could get quite argumentative after a few drinks. It amused him that he could sometimes wake up with no recollection of how he had got home from his club the night before. But one Sunday he was horrified on waking to discover the living room furniture scattered about, and his wife not in the house. His memory was a blank. He was afraid he had been violent to his wife. He had not, but the experience was terrifying and became a turning point in his life.

'One for the way home'

PROBLEMS IN FAMILIES

The person who is a regular drinker devotes time, energy and money to drinking. Sometimes this leaves the family short, not just of money, but of what he or she could be bringing to family life. Father forgets when he promised his son an outing. Mother loses interest in her teenagers. The drinking becomes a sore point. Marriages become more empty; arguments about drink take over as the chief topic of conversation – except in those families where no-one dares say anything about it for fear of causing a row. An affectionate wife turns cold and hostile, and bitter at her husband living only for the pub. A kind, considerate husband grows aloof and distant – ashamed, perhaps disgusted and insulted, by his wife's drinking. Children lose respect, becoming defiant, sulky and unhappy. They start to do poorly at school. (See Chapter 9.)

PROBLEMS AT WORK

Odd days off, occasionally arriving late, or frequent sick lines (for those hangovers and stomach upsets) are overlooked by many employers. But a day of reckoning may arise and to lose a job in this way can be demoralising. Some, but not all, employers want to be helpful and suspend disciplinary action if an employee with a drinking problem is determined to do something about it. After all, the employee is often a highly trained and valuable member of staff and it is not in the employer's interest to lose him or her.

Drinkers often think no-one at work notices that, for example, they always drink at lunchtime or have alcohol on their breath in the morning from last night's drinking. They may be surprised that everyone knows, long before they themselves began to think they were drinking too much.

TROUBLE WITH THE LAW

Three pints of beer, or three 'doubles' of spirits, is sufficient to send the alcohol level in the blood over the legal limit for driving (80 milligrammes in 100 millilitres of blood in the UK; 50 milligrammes per 100 millilitres in Australia). The penalty is disqualification from driving and a fine. People who drink a lot build up a tolerance, that is they are not so obviously affected by drink. But the same amount of alcohol still gives the same blood alcohol reading.

One unit of alcohol (half a pint of beer or a single measure of spirits) takes roughly one hour to leave the body. Someone who drinks half a bottle of spirits (375 millilitres) or seven pints of beer (i.e. 14–15 units) in the evening is likely to be over the legal limit for driving at 8 a.m. next day. In many countries, including the UK, offenders detected with a blood or breath alcohol above certain fairly high levels are required to pass a medical examination with special blood tests if they wish to regain their licence. This is to assess whether or not they have changed their drinking habits.

Being publicly drunk can be an offence, especially if the person causes a nuisance. Some towns provide places where drunk people can be taken to sober up instead of being taken into custody. Usually, though, the result is an uncomfortable and undignified night in the cells and a court appearance in the morning. It is also an offence to be drunk when in charge of a child.

IN WHAT WAY CAN ALCOHOL DAMAGE HEALTH?

This diagram shows the ways in which moderate to heavy drinking over months or years affects the body:

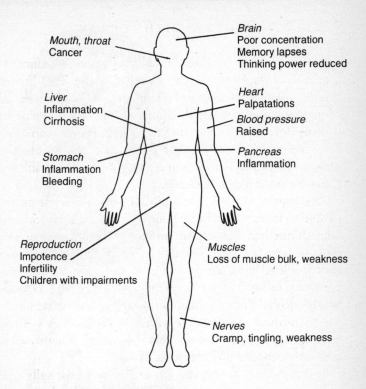

Figure 2 Parts of the body affected by alcohol

The brain

Intelligence does not stop someone from becoming dependent on alcohol: authors, lawyers, doctors and professors are as vulnerable as the rest of us. However, drinking can cause a decline in intelligence and many problem drinkers cope less well with tests of thinking than they should do, given their previously known level of intelligence. There can even be shrinkage of the brain, as the photographs in Figure 3 show. This may be one reason why some excessive drinkers often

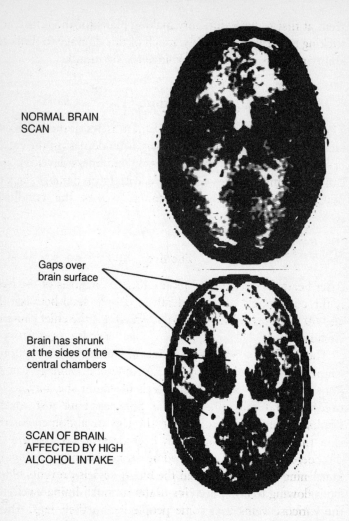

NORMAL BRAIN
SCAN

Gaps over
brain surface

Brain has shrunk
at the sides of the
central chambers

SCAN OF BRAIN
AFFECTED BY HIGH
ALCOHOL INTAKE

*Figure 3 Heavy drinking affects intelligence and can cause shrinkage of the
brain. This can happen in people who are otherwise in good health and seem
normal. The top scan shows a normal brain. The black border is the skull
bone; the shaded area is brain; the white is fluid. The lower scan shows too
much white. The brain tissue round the central fluid-containing chambers has
shrunk, and there are gaps over the surface where shrinking has occurred.*

seem at first to have difficulty making plans for the future and sticking to them. Fortunately, much of this damage to thinking ability recovers if alcohol is avoided for six months.

Neuritis

The nerves that travel to the skin and muscles of the limbs can be damaged. At first this only shows as tenderness in the calves or cramp. Later, pins and needles or numbness develops and can be painful. The legs weaken. As with brain damage, lack of nourishment, especially B vitamins, makes the condition worse.

The liver

After heart disease, cancer and accidents, cirrhosis of the liver is the commonest cause of death in people aged between 20 and 60 in industrialised countries. Alcohol is the chief cause of cirrhosis.

The liver is the processing plant on which the body's nourishment and chemistry depend. Considerable damage can be done to it before the individual feels ill. He or she may notice tiredness and may put down a poor appetite just to the drinking. Later, fluid collects in the legs or abdomen, or the skin turns yellow. Death from liver disease may be due to disordered chemistry, or bleeding from the stomach lining. Hardening in the liver round the blood vessels prevents blood from flowing freely. The veins in the stomach lining swell like the varicose veins that some people get in their legs. These veins can bleed and the bleeding can be impossible to stop.

A doctor is usually able to tell by examining you and taking blood tests whether or not you have liver disease. Fortunately, people with early alcoholic liver disease who stop drinking have a 90 per cent chance of a normal life expectancy.

However, medical treatment can achieve little or nothing if drinking continues. Death invariably follows.

The digestive system

A night's heavy drinking may cause irritation of the stomach, with vomiting or bleeding. Vomited blood can be red, or brown like coffee grounds. Alcohol worsens any tendency to stomach or duodenal ulcers. In some people diarrhoea may be caused by alcohol. There is often slight damage to the intestine, which means that vitamins in food are not properly absorbed. Heavy drinkers also run short of vitamins if they don't eat proper meals.

The pancreas lies behind the stomach and makes digestive juices and insulin. It may be damaged by alcohol, causing a painful condition called pancreatitis.

Heavy drinkers are liable to cancer in the mouth, throat and gullet.

The heart

Alcohol can cause the heart to beat irregularly or too quickly. The heart feels as if it is fluttering or gives a bumping or wobbling feeling in the chest. High blood pressure and strokes are also connected with heavy drinking. Alcohol weakens muscles and this can include the heart.

Sex

Does alcohol increase sexual ability? Alcohol may make us feel less inhibited and apparently keener on sex. However, in men alcohol may cause impotence. This is because a large dose of alcohol affects the nerves necessary for an erection. If this has happened once or twice a man may become worried about his sexual ability and the sure way for a man to be unable to keep an erection is to worry about it. This is what the adverts do not say: the effect of such-and-such a drink can indeed be shattering! Alcohol reduces male hormone levels, which reduces the sex drive and also reduces the chance of fathering a child.

The complexion and figure

A blotchy complexion is common in regular drinkers and, if liver disease is developing, tiny spidery sets of blood vessels may appear on the face.

An alcoholic drink usually contains about 100 calories, but some drinkers lose weight because alcohol dulls their appetite. Those who continue to eat normally put on weight but can still be short of vitamins.

Alcohol and women's health

Women become intoxicated after drinking smaller quantities of alcohol than are needed to produce intoxication in men. This is partly because for a given body weight, a woman has less body water to dilute the alcohol. Also, less of the alcohol is broken down in the woman's stomach lining than in the man's, so more enters her blood stream.

Women dependent on alcohol have a higher death rate than men with the problem. Suicide and accidents contribute to this. The woman's liver is also likely to develop cirrhosis earlier than a man's, and at a lower intake of alcohol.

Breast cancer is, like liver cirrhosis, a leading cause of death in women aged 30–50, and in recent years studies suggest that heavy drinking may have contributed to breast cancer in some women.

Alcohol and pregnancy

Sometimes, heavy drinking causes hormone disturbance, with irregular periods and failure to conceive. It can cause the menopause to start earlier. Women who drink heavily in pregnancy increase the chance that their babies will be small, frail, backward or even deformed. Some studies show that it can be harmful to the unborn child if the mother drinks even lightly, though some studies do not. It is probably best to be safe and avoid all alcohol (and cigarettes) during pregnancy.

DEPENDENCE ON ALCOHOL

Some people feel they regularly need a drink at certain times or in certain situations. Some rely on alcohol in the belief that it gets rid of tension or depression. Some depend on it to dull reality. For some, drinking has simply become such a habit

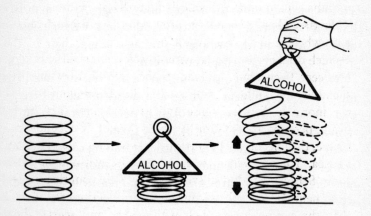

Figure 4 Think of the nervous system as a spring. Alcohol is like a heavy weight pressing down on the spring. When the weight is removed the spring is unstable and rebounds.

that they find their routine impossible to change. These people are *psychologically dependent*. Their drinking is linked to certain triggers. Triggers may be inner emotions, such as depression or frustration, so that whenever they feel that way they find themselves thinking of a drink. Triggers can also be more ordinary: passing a certain pub on the way home may set off the train of thought, or preparing the evening meal or sitting in a chair watching TV. Ordinary habits can become very fixed when a drug is involved – and alcohol is a drug.

Alcohol is a drug which, like heroin, causes *chemical dependence*. If alcohol is taken regularly the nervous system (the brain and its many connections) gets used to it. The nerve cells adapt. When alcohol is not there, or is there but in lower amounts, these adaptations are suddenly excessive because they are not needed. This gives a rebound effect. This rebound effect depends on how much alcohol has been drunk and for how long. Individuals vary. Five pints of beer (i.e. five double measures of spirits, or eight or nine glasses of wine or sherry – see chart on p. 18) spread throughout the day for several months will produce chemical dependence in most people. Then the individual is out of sorts and restless for three or four days when he or she stops drinking.

Such drinkers notice that without alcohol it is difficult to get to sleep. Even after drinking in the evening they may find themselves waking at 3 or 4 a.m. – another rebound effect. In the morning they feel tense and irritable until they have a drink, perhaps at lunchtime, perhaps sooner. If dependence is severe, the tension is accompanied by sweating, trembling and nausea. These discomforts are also called withdrawal symptoms. Serious withdrawal symptoms include vomiting, fearfulness, palpitations, epileptic fits and DTs (delirium tremens). In DTs the person loses touch with reality and sees or hears things that are not there.

The carry-over effect

People who have been chemically dependent on alcohol, and then abstain for a period, are liable to make themselves dependent on alcohol again surprisingly rapidly if they recommence drinking. It may have taken several years' drinking for them to get to the point of chemical dependence, but on the second occasion the symptoms of dependence reappear much more quickly, sometimes after a week or two or even less. Even one or two days of moderate drinking are followed by the familiar and unpleasant shakiness, sickness and urge to take more alcohol. The tendency to dependence is carried over from the earlier period. Many people are affected in this way.

Some laboratory breeds of mice and rats are surprisingly likely to become dependent on alcohol if given access to it. Experiments have shown they experience the same carry-over effect that occurs in alcohol-dependent humans. Animals already made dependent on alcohol will, after a period of abstinence, develop the same tendency to withdrawal symptoms on a lower dose and after fewer days of exposure to alcohol, than after their first period of dependence or compared to other animals of the same breed.

Is dependence on alcohol an illness?

If someone has become dependent on alcohol, there are changes in the brain cells as well as in their habitual way of reacting to life. Such people find it more difficult than the rest of us to control whether or not they drink and how much they drink. In this way dependence on alcohol can be called an illness. *However, it is essential that they try to control their drinking. Their recovery will depend on how hard they try, as well as on how much help they receive.*

AM I DRINKING TOO MUCH?

If you have any of the troubles already mentioned you are drinking too much, if not all the time, at least some of the time.

But assuming all is well, you feel fine and no-one is complaining, are there any signals you should look out for?

1. Are you becoming dependent? – Are there certain situations when you always need a drink, for example before every social engagement, or when under pressure? Is your nervous system getting so used to alcohol that two pints of beer or four drinks have no effect on you? Do you need one or two more drinks than your friends?

½ pint ordinary lager or beer

1 single of spirits

=

= 1 unit

1 glass sherry

1 glass wine

=

Figure 5 Alcohol content of various beverages. Each of the above contains the same amount of alcohol — 1 unit (8 grams).

2. Have you tried already to limit your drinking and failed? Perhaps you simply switched to another type of drink, or you managed for a while but it crept up again? (See the drinks chart below.)

3. Have you got problems (family, money, work) which you have been ignoring or blaming on something else, but which could be due partly to your drinking or how you behave when you have been drinking?

4. Has a blood test from your family doctor shown an abnormality?

5. Are you drinking to solve a problem? You may rapidly find yourself drinking too much – and end up with two problems!

The Drinks Chart: the alcohol content in various drinks

Ordinary beer and lager, sweet stout	½ pint	about 1 unit
Export beer, stout	1 pint	about 2½ units
'Special' lager, 'diet' lager	½ pint	2 units
	16oz can	3 units
Cider (strength varies)	½ pint	1-2 units
Table wine	1 bottle (75 cl)	8 units
Sherry, port, 'tonic wine', vermouth	1 bottle (75 cl)	14 units
Spirits (gin, whisky, vodka, liqueurs, Pimms, aniseed drinks such as Pernod)	1 bottle (75 cl)	30 units

3

Can anyone develop a drinking problem?

Looking at our changing drinking habits in the last 200 years, and at the patterns in different countries, it seems that when alcohol is relatively cheap and drinking is part of everyday life,

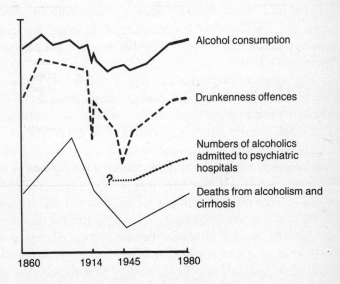

Figure 6 The number of people with drinking problems depends on the national level of drinking.

more people run into difficulties with it. France for example has a high rate of alcoholism: nearly every third hospital bed has a patient suffering from some hazard of drinking. The graph in Figure 6 shows how the number of people with drinking problems varies when the national level of drinking varies. However, some of us are more likely to develop a problem than others.

DOES PROBLEM DRINKING RUN IN FAMILIES?

Yes. A man or woman whose father or mother had an alcohol problem has a high risk of following in their footsteps. As teenagers we vow we will never be like Father or Mother, but we wake up one day in adult life to discover that in some ways we are the image of them. A tense worrying nature can be handed on. We may have a tendency to cope with stress in the same way a parent did. Or perhaps what is passed from parent to child is something to do with the way alcohol affects the brain or the body.

The scientific background to this is as follows. Twins who are identical have identical genes, that is, their basic body chemistry is the same. There are also twins who are non-ident-ical – born at the same time but no more alike than pairs of brothers and sisters. Identical twins grow up with drinking habits which tend to be similar, more so than those of non-identical twins, and more so than can be due to their being more in each other's company. Some, but not all, studies of twins find a genetic (hereditary) factor not just for the amount of drinking but for alcohol dependence too. When a parent with an alcohol problem has given up his or her child for adop-tion when the child was little, we find that the child is more likely to have an alcohol problem than other children in the family where he or she was brought up, showing that something to do with drink problems was passed on from the biological parent.

DO SOME JOBS PUT YOU AT RISK?

Drinking problems are commoner in people from certain occupations:

- Jobs where alcohol is readily available and drinking is part of the way of life (the drink trade, sales representatives, certain company directors).
- Jobs where people are away from their families (at sea, in the armed services, salesmen, the construction industry).
- Jobs where there is relatively little supervision (lawyers, doctors, journalists).

As you might expect, some of these jobs attract people who already drink regularly.

IS PERSONALITY IMPORTANT?

It is often successful, social, outgoing people who turn out in their 30s and 40s to have developed a drink problem. They may then become depressed, tense, suspicious or worried; but this is the result of alcohol and the trouble that has piled up. Occasionally tendencies to worrying, depression or feelings of inferiority have been there since adolescence and drinking has been an unsuccessful attempt to banish those feelings. However, people with a drink problem do not necessarily have some deeply buried twist in their personalities. Once they have stopped drinking, life becomes satisfying and productive again.

IS STRESS IMPORTANT?

People mean different things by the word stress. To some it conjures up busy executives besieged by unfinished paperwork, unable to delegate, who do not take time out to relax. They may use alcohol to unwind at 6 p.m. without necessarily improving their tempers with families in the evening – if they get home in time to see them.

To others stress means the bickering and nagging in an unfortunate marriage; the burden of coping unsupported with unruly children; the frustration and demoralisation of unemployment; or the worry of looking after an elderly parent.

Bereavement, or a marriage breaking up, particularly for the person with few relatives or friends, can cause prolonged pain. Sometimes people drink to dull this pain.

All of these kinds of stress (and many others) can contribute to a drinking problem. However, these are difficulties which often are made gradually worse in the long run by drinking. They are sometimes difficulties which with careful reflection, and perhaps guidance, could be rapidly overcome by a change in attitude or in one's way of reacting. (More of this in Chapter 6.)

Occasionally, stresses are more imaginary than real. They are convenient excuses for putting off doing something about a deeply engrained habit, which has now become troublesome. People often say: 'It's my boss [or my wife] who makes me drink,' when in truth it is the drinking and the behaviour that goes with it that has made the boss or the spouse critical.

Nobody is ever responsible for another person's drinking. We always have choices as to how we react to another person's behaviour. We do not have to respond in destructive ways.

ARE THE YOUNG IMMUNE?

Socialising and nights out almost always involve drinking, so it is not surprising that many people in their teens and 20s have a spell when they are drinking a lot. Usually marriage and young children change all that! Or other interests develop or the job makes new demands. But the young person whose habits have become very set, and who begins drinking more than three or four units (see page 18) every day in addition to social outings is at risk of becoming dependent on alcohol – even if everything else in life is going well. *Specially at risk is the young person who has not found satisfaction in personal relationships or a job and who makes drinking his or her main hobby. He or she is best to be careful about alcohol and look into other ways of making life more exciting and more enjoyable.* (See Chapter 8 on Teenagers.)

CAN THE ELDERLY BE AFFECTED?

The price of alcohol is one reason why the over-70s appear less often in the statistics. However, elderly people can become

dependent on alcohol, sometimes apparently out of the blue. Depression may be the cause, or the death or disablement of husband or wife. Falls and fractures (so dangerous in the elderly) are sometimes the consequence of excessive drinking. Premature senility is another hazard. As we get older, alcohol more easily affects our intelligence as well as our balance mechanism.

4

Should I change my drinking pattern?

Try making a balance sheet showing in one column the good things about your drinking and in the other column the negative things, the drawbacks of your drinking.

The good things	*The drawbacks*
e.g. I enjoy the taste It's how I meet friends It helps me relax I feel I get on better with people when I've had a drink I feel less shy with the opposite sex	e.g. It's costing too much It's upsetting the family Drink is affecting my work I get tired afterwards Sex isn't so good I'm worried about my liver, . . . my brain etc.

Of course there have been, and probably still are, many good points about drinking. But a time may come when these are outweighed by the problems it causes. If the columns don't balance, a decision to do something about your drinking is logically the next step. Try to be honest, with yourself at least.

BUT IS THE DRINKING THE REAL TROUBLE?

'Drink isn't my problem, it's the answer to my problems.' If a person has begun to drink in an attempt to solve a problem it can be very hard for him or her to see that alcohol has become a problem in itself. Though alcohol helps tense people to relax, regular drinking increases tension because of the frequent minor 'withdrawal effects' (see page 15). Though alcohol may seem a stimulant, it achieves this effect by releasing inhibitions. For a short time you may feel 'freer'. However, the depressing effect lasts longer than the stimulant effect. Though enough alcohol dulls mental as well as physical pain, it does this by depressing the nervous system – and mental depression makes pain worse. These are some of the reasons why drinking to solve mental distress can actually worsen it.

OR IS THE REAL PROBLEM MY JOB? ... OR MY PARTNER? ... OR MY FAMILY?

Of course there may be difficulties with colleagues, husband, wife, parents. Alcohol, or the friendly atmosphere of the pub, can provide a welcome escape but seldom an answer. Perhaps your partner/parent/employer is not going to change anyhow. Putting the blame on them is not going to improve anything.

... AND WHO SAYS SO?

Most of us get irritated if someone makes critical comments about our habits or lifestyle. It is worse if we feel guilty or ashamed already. An angry retort from us may make the critic conveniently back off.

Sometimes, however, we need others to help us see things

the way they really are. Most of us can shut out from our minds things we did that we would rather forget. Our memory of what happened on drinking days is particularly liable to be patchy.

I'M AT MY BEST WHEN DRINKING

Occasionally people say: 'I am someone who needs it – I'm at my best when I've had a few. It adds a new dimension to my life. Look at the poets, painters, composers who were drinkers; look at Winston Churchill.' That may be. But if you have a problem in your life, concentrate on that, not the next person. It's not very creative to make yourself ill through drinking.

I'LL LOSE MY ONLY PLEASURE IN LIFE

It's a matter of weighing up the advantages against the dis-advantages of your drinking. Life without your style of drinking IS possible. Lots of people have gone along the path you are now contemplating.

SHOULD I JUST CUT DOWN, OR STOP ALTOGETHER?

Some problem drinkers decide to continue to drink and manage to avoid further problems. They make a radical change, not only reducing what they drink on any one occasion (e.g. never more than two or three drinks), but also cut back on how often they drink (e.g. never more than two or three times per week).

By all means try reducing rather than stopping. If it does not work, be honest and avoid looking for excuses. In our experience, and according to research findings, *abstinence is essential if any of the following apply to you*:

- If you have had symptoms of dependence for several months or more (see page 14).
- If your husband or wife is not in agreement with your plans for limited drinking (i.e. if any drinking sets up tension).
- If you tend to be someone who is easily upset, or does things very much on the spur of the moment.
- If you are not good at making rules for yourself: with abstinence there is one simple rule for every occasion – no alcohol – and that is easy for your family and friends to understand too.

'*Some people just never learn*'

- If you have damaged any of the body's organs (such as the liver) through drinking.

If you are going for cutting down rather than abstinence read pages 41–43 and check the stories of Andrew and Bill.

Many people find it easier and more effective to stop altogether, because they can never be sure how a drinking occasion will end. Tom is typical of a number of people with drinking problems. He writes: 'Sometimes, indeed quite often, I could and did drink without any bad reactions, but I could never be *sure* that tonight was not going to be the night when I lost control of myself. It was like playing Russian roulette with a bottle instead of a gun. Every so often I pulled out the loaded chamber, and blew my brains out.'

Or you may find that although single drinking occasions never become excessive, there is a gradual tendency for drinking to increase considerably over a few weeks – those first days when drinking is light and pleasant are the thin edge of a wedge. Raymond Chandler, the detective thriller writer, in a letter to a friend, saw it like this: 'I have been sober now for some weeks – absolutely bone-dry sober. Dull as it may be, I intend to remain that way. Something in my chemistry will no longer accept alcohol. There is some sort of chain reaction. I start off with a drink of white wine and end up drinking two bottles of Scotch a day.'

The willow and the oak

You probably remember the story of the willow and the oak tree. A gale blew up and the willow bowed over but the oak tried to stand straight without bending and was uprooted. If it has become too difficult to be certain that your drinking can always be controlled then it is best to admit it. To keep on trying to prove to yourself that you can master it, is to risk being uprooted like the oak.

STOP? ... HOW LONG FOR?

Some people decide to stop for ever, others stop for a while and recommence limited drinking once the stresses and strains of the problem period have diminished, the brain has cleared and constructive thinking is again possible. Drinking again is safer if the new pattern is totally different from the old pattern (i.e. when, where and with whom). But why not cross this bridge when you come to it? Leave it to next year to worry about whether or not to drink next year. Take a day at a time. The important thing is to have decided to do something about it now.

I SEE ALL THIS, BUT IT DOES NOT APPLY TO ME

Of course perhaps none of this applies to you. But because none of us likes to make a critical examination of ourselves, just give this chapter a moment's reflection for two reasons:

1. To be sure you are seeing yourself as others see you.
2. To check whether your real objection is to do with a fear of losing face. ('No-one is going to convince me I've got a drink problem').

Take for example Ian, a bank branch manager who was temporarily suspended from his job. He wrote: 'The major problem is to realise that you have a problem. I knew deep down that I had; but kept saying that I had had a drink today because of some stress and that tomorrow I would not have the stress – but I still had that drink ... When things got out of hand and I was forced to admit it I was ashamed. On my first visit to my doctor I told him it was a minor problem, which was a lie. As soon as I was able to admit to him that the problem was a real problem the "cure" began.'

5

How to succeed

PREPARING FOR CHANGE

The big question is – do you really want to change your drinking pattern? If you really do, you will probably succeed. Making up your mind is what counts.

I've tried before but I could not stick to it

Lots of people try several times before altering their drinking. But the circumstances are never exactly the same twice. If you fear you will miss drink greatly, remember that the desire usually gets less the longer you manage without it.

If I stop drinking spirits will that be sufficient?

If your carefully considered aim is only to cut down, it may be a useful strategy to move to a dilute form of alcohol such as shandy or ordinary lager. You can make that sort of drink last longer. However, half a pint of lager contains as much alcohol as a single of spirits. And it is a fact that men and women who have drunk only ordinary beer, lager or cider have died of alcoholism. So keep an honest eye on your total intake.

Be clear about your reasons

Think through the reasons for changing your drinking habits. You might decide: 'my health will improve', or 'I'll save some money' (why not work out how much?), or 'my family will be happier' or 'I'll get on better at work'. Why not take a sheet of paper now and write down your own reasons?

Be clear about your decision

Try to be absolutely clear about the limits you are setting yourself. Of if you decide to stop, set a target (a month ... a week ... or just a day) and fix a day to check up on how it went, to reward yourself and to set the next target. Tell your decision to a friend or someone in the family and make an agreement to let them know how you manage. Plan to save the money you don't spend and put it towards something to look forward to – a holiday, for example. At present prices, five cans of beer a day for two months could pay for a week's holiday in the sun, including the flight.

Planning ahead

Don't let tricky situations catch you out. Plan in advance what you will do if you meet one of your 'triggers' (see page 15).

If time is likely to weigh heavily on you at first, think ahead to what you might do. Maybe you like reading, crosswords, listening to music or do-it-yourself? There are more suggestions on page 38.

Do I need special help?

Yes – if you have tried several times before and failed.

Yes – if you have no-one close to check with you on your progress.

Yes – if you have had serious withdrawal symptoms in the recent past (fits, hallucinations, or severe shaking).

Yes – if you feel afraid of a future without alcohol because it has been your only escape from intolerable worries or fears.

Caution: If you are going for help merely to pacify your family, your employer or your conscience, think twice. If that is the case you probably won't be putting much into your treatment, and so you won't get much out of it. Go for yourself, because YOU WANT to do something about your drinking and your life.

IMMEDIATE SURVIVAL – THE FIRST WEEK

Will I have withdrawal symptoms?

The more you have been drinking in the past two or three weeks, the more severe the withdrawal symptoms are likely to be. Below 14 units (i.e. half a bottle of spirits or seven pints of ordinary strength beer) per day, these 'rebound' symptoms are unlikely to require medical observation. Above that level, symptoms may be severe. Individuals react differently. Symptoms are less if you cut down gradually over four or five days instead of stopping abruptly.

Restlessness, trembling and inability to sleep are worst 24 to 48 hours after the last drink and improve gradually so that physical discomfort has passed after roughly a week. If a doctor assesses that withdrawal symptoms are likely to be severe he or she may prescribe tranquillizers. You start taking the pills on the day you stop drinking, reduce gradually over 4 to 7 days and then stop taking them.

What should I eat and drink?

Don't miss meals – even if you are not hungry try to eat something. Your appetite will return. If your stomach is uncomfortable, milk may be soothing. Vitamin shortages need to be replaced as soon as possible. Drink plenty of fruit juice, squash, sodas or water. Don't drink more than two cups of ordinary coffee or four cups of tea per day – these contain caffeine which disturbs sleep and causes nervousness.

How can I relax during this period?

Face up to it – it may be difficult. We say more about this on page 39. Meantime, here are some tips:

- Avoid stress. It may be best to take a week off work. Change your routine.

'Getting busy round the house'

- Take relaxing warm baths.
- Listen to your favourite kind of music.
- Go for walks.
- Get busy round the house.
- Above all, do something – anything – that will distract you from the thought that you are tense or need a drink.
- Avoid negative thinking (see pages 55–58).

Sleep

You are bound to sleep less well, so be prepared for this. But lack of sleep does not seriously harm you. Your sleep pattern will return to normal in a month or so, if not sooner. It is better not to take sleeping pills, so that your normal sleep rhythm can return. Don't go to sleep in front of the TV. Go to bed very late, read a book or paper, do a jigsaw-puzzle, and have a bedtime snack or warm milky drink. Or you can buy cassette tapes that talk you through relaxation and help you to sleep; you will find these in bookshops.

THE FIRST FEW MONTHS

How do I handle parties, pubs and other drinking occasions?

Many people who regularly drink alcohol feel that if they stop they will be abnormal or outcasts. It is hard to realise at first that there are millions of people who do not touch alcohol. Their reasons vary: health, religion, or simply a dislike of the taste or the effect alcohol has on them. But it is common to feel under some pressure if you return to drinking company. It is best to avoid drinking situations at first, until you have a firm new identity as a 'light drinker' or a 'non-drinker'. Changing your routine is also important because now is the ideal time to start a new spare-time activity which does not revolve around drinking.

What do I say to people?

It is best to tell people right away that you have decided on a major change in your drinking. People will then be less likely to misunderstand or be offended when you refuse a drink, less likely to try to persuade you to change your mind, and less likely to put pressure on you by joking about your not drinking. Many will admire your control. They will also be more likely to get soft drinks in when you visit, or order you a soft drink at the bar.

Whom to tell?

You should at least tell family, close friends and drinking companions. They are likely to be understanding because they may already know there is a problem and will be relieved to talk about it.

When to tell?

As soon as possible. Putting it off makes it harder. With drinking companions try to choose a moment when they are not drinking – they are more likely to take your seriously!

How to say it

It has to sound as if you mean it. People will only take you seriously if you have obviously made your mind up. Don't let people think it's temporary – they will soon be wondering when they should start offering you your usual drink again.

For example: 'I've been ill recently and I've been told I'll be all right as long as I always avoid alcohol. There's something wrong with my stomach (or liver) and it reacts very badly to alcohol now, even small amounts. I've *got* to stay off it so it helps if no-one offers me a drink.' Or, 'I find one or two drinks isn't any good to me, so I don't drink at all now.'

There are bound to be occasions, socially or in the course of business, when a quick excuse is needed: 'No thanks, I'm driving,' or 'I'm on pills and alcohol is out,' or else 'I've got to keep a clear head for some desk work this afternoon.'

But *excuses wear thin, so where you can tell the truth* – '*No thanks, I don't drink.*'

YOU HAVE A RIGHT TO SAY 'NO'.

What do I ask for if offered a drink?

If you find a non-alcoholic drink you like, stick to it – your friends will soon know to get it for you without being asked. Is low alcohol lager ('Clausthaler', 'Kaliber', etc.) a good choice? If cold these lagers are a refreshing non-sweet drink. But beware living out the illusion that you are still one of the beer-drinking lads – it may be time you changed that image of yourself! Do you need to make out to people that you are still drinking? Mineral waters ('Perrier' etc) with ice are fashionable, not sweet – and free of calories. Beware tonic wine, ginger wine and cider: all contain alcohol.

Suppose I still feel awkward in drinking company?

People are usually helpful if you are honest with them. Don't feel you have to apologise for not drinking. Your health and well-being are what is important – don't let anyone interfere with that. You don't have to please anyone else.

Should I keep alcohol in the house?

If you live with family or friends who drink occasionally then the atmosphere may be easier if alcoholic drinks are not removed from the house. However, if you live alone, or if your drinking was done in secret, then it is wise to remove alcohol from the home.

What can I put in place of alcohol?

The answer to this depends on what function drinking has had in your life.

If drinking has been the main way of using your spare time, then time may weigh heavily when you stop. Avoid getting bored. Here are a few suggestions:

- Get busy round the house.
- Join the public library, not just for books but to keep in touch with the notices showing what's on in your locality.
- Acquire a pet.
- Take an evening class or correspondence course.
- Take up a new hobby (you may need a few tries) – if equipment is expensive remember that you are saving money if you are drinking less.
- Make a commitment to the Church or a voluntary body.

Our clients have reported getting involved in gardening; reading; going to the cinema; learning massage; taking up computer games; learning gourmet cooking; rock polishing; learning to swim, which they did not manage as a child; playing chess; canoeing; teaching reading to adult late-learners; camping; cycling; rebuilding motor cycles; tapestry, quilting; knitting; joining a choir; working in a charity shop; helping at Riding for the Disabled; renovating old furniture; hospital volunteer driving; and befriending a mentally handi-capped person.

If drinking has been a way of enjoying company, a new spare-time activity is the best way to meet a new circle of friends. Evening classes are often friendly. Alcoholics Anonymous and the local Councils on Alcoholism (see chapter 14) are ways of getting to know people in the same boat. (Loneliness is discussed on page 51).

Get fit

You will feel better in yourself if you are physically in good condition and taking regular exercise. Take some exercise every day, even if it is only walking. Local authorities offer a range of sporting facilities and keep-fit classes, with reduced rates for the unemployed or elderly. Keep fit and dance classes are also a way of meeting people.

Teach yourself to relax

There are various methods of learning to relax, e.g. lie down or sit comfortably in a chair and systematically tense and relax each set of muscles in your body one by one. Start with your feet, move on to your calves and so on up your body. To relax a tense muscle, tighten it hard, hold it for three seconds, then let it go floppy and loose. Work over your whole body, finishing with the face and scalp. Your breathing should be slow and fairly deep. The breath out is slow and extended, with the lower jaw relaxed and the mouth open. Tense on the in-breath and let go on the out-breath.

Sometimes simply sitting in a chair with your legs and arms resting and counting your breaths will relax you. If your mind goes on to other things, go back to counting your breaths to stop 'mind chatter', going over all those useless conversations about what might have been, or might be.

KEEPING IT UP

1. Don't let what others do or say be an excuse for drinking. *No-one but yourself is responsible for your drinking. You make the decisions.*
2. Avoid self-pity and dwelling on the past. (If you suffer from attacks of 'poor-me' read page 49.)
3. Don't be taken in. If you chose to stop or were advised to and found it easy, you may catch yourself thinking you could now have the odd drink and stop again whenever you want to. Take care. There's probably a part of you that wants to get back to the old pattern again and it will produce plenty of reasons: 'One won't hurt' ... 'I deserve a reward' ... 'It's a holiday weekend' and so on.
4. Give yourself a reward. As Helen (page 108) said, 'It's a good idea to spoil oneself a little. For instance, instead of buying a bottle of sherry or wine, I treated myself to a new lipstick or perfume.' You may find your savings going up quite fast if you have stopped drinking. We have seen clients buying themselves another car or having an expensive holiday in a matter of months.
5. Immunise yourself against the urge to drink. Reaffirm your reasons for deciding to avoid alcohol. List in your mind, or on paper, the bad things about your drinking and the good things about not drinking.
6. Use self-talk (inner speech), the more catchy the better: 'One day at a time.' 'First things first.' 'Be positive.' Write these phrases on some cards to keep in your wallet or handbag, or on the mantelpiece.*
7. Practise rational self-talk: 'I decided not to drink. I have the sense not to drink.' 'I'm making a melodrama of this. I

---

* Just because this smacks of platitudes does not make it less useful.

don't hurt *that* much.' 'Each time I give way to impulsive behaviour I give away control of my life.'

8. If you are drinking to give yourself Dutch courage, begin to see that most people have a fear of change. Feel the fear and do it anyway – this is the only way to build confidence. Go right through with it, without alcohol, and find that you are able to cope after all.

9. Beware over-confidence and complacency.

NORMAL DRINKING?

You may have decided from the start that your aim is to train yourself to be a normal drinker. Check first on page 28 to see if you score on any of the items that make abstinence essential. Take care! This can be a recipe for disaster. If you wish to aim for normal drinking, it is vital to make firm rules for yourself such as:

- A rule about when and how much you will drink. 'Saturdays only' or 'never drink on more than two days in a row and never at lunchtimes' or 'maximum four units on any day (i.e. two pints of ordinary lager – see page 17) or six units at a celebration.'

- Make your drinks last (sip don't gulp); start with one or two non-alcoholic drinks.

- Buy your own drinks; avoid buying rounds. This is not always easy. But if you find yourself in bars sometimes, try buying your own drink as soon as you arrive before you are offered one. Or say to companions that you'll be leaving soon and so would rather just buy your own. Sometimes the others are glad not to be caught up in round-buying – you probably occasionally felt that way yourself.

- Avoid drinking on an empty stomach.
- Avoid company where there is heavy drinking.
- Don't drink when depressed or angry.
- Keep a diary of your consumption to see if you are keeping to your rules.
- Be honest with yourself – get someone (a relation or a specialist) to help you see how your experiment is doing.

Here are two accounts which illustrate some of the pitfalls and possibilities:

Bill succeeded at 'normal drinking'. He had been a steady pen-pusher at head office. He was well liked, though never the life and soul of the party. He used to go to the White Horse pub each day after work, have two or three pints of beer and put the world to rights. Saturday and Sunday lunch-times were favourite drinking occasions when he met old friends and arranged fishing trips. Then he was promoted. He found the new job a strain. There were too many telephone calls, too many decisions. By lunchtime he often felt tense and would unwind in the pub. By 5 p.m. he was ready for another three pints and frequently this was four to five. His wife disliked him arriving home late, intoxicated and irritable, and going straight to sleep in front of the TV. At work in the afternoons he made mistakes and was edgy. His manager asked him to see a doctor about his nerves and his drinking. He had only once been shaky in the morning, after a New Year celebration, and had never had other withdrawal symptoms. He decided to stop drinking completely and took Antabuse (see page 107) for eight weeks. He asked for a transfer to another department, changed his route home from work so that he did not pass his pub, and decided each Saturday to go shopping with his wife and have lunch in town. When three months had passed, he and his wife discussed the possibility of him drinking again. With her full agreement, though she was nervous about it at first, he began having beer on their Saturday lunch outings (two pints maximum) and either Sunday lunchtime or evening (but not both) went to his pub for an hour before closing time for two pints. For a period he recorded in a diary what he had to drink. Now, three years later, he seldom deviates from his new pattern of drinking. He consciously avoids drinking on weekdays except on holiday. His wife is no longer worried about his drinking and he is pleased with the way things are going.

Andrew's story is different. At the age of 28 he took a job as a salesman. He began regularly drinking at lunchtime, and although at first this was just one or two drinks, after a year in the job it was three or four. He was away from home often and in the evening he would have seven or eight drinks. Without alcohol in the evening he had difficulty sleeping. Without alcohol by 12 noon he was tense and the slightest stress made him sweat. Soon he was taking a mid-morning drink, by organising his day so that he could either visit a customer who would offer him a whisky, or else finish his visits early and go to a pub where he was well known. Without that drink his hand would tremble. One day he was charged by the police for drinking and driving. He had a discussion with his wife, and decided to stop completely. He did so for six weeks and then began accepting lunchtime drinks again. He soon noticed he always wanted a 5 p.m. drink if he had had alcohol at lunchtime, and he always needed a 10 p.m. drink if he had been drinking at 5 p.m. Within ten weeks his shakiness had returned. His drinking seemed to be as heavy as ever. He had another charge for drinking and driving and because it involved a serious accident he spent a night in custody. On returning home from court after having had no alcohol for 24 hours he felt frightened and thought people were following him and talking about him. He was shaking all over. Tranquillizers got him through this period and he abstained from drink for a month. But when he heard he was to lose his job he felt very sorry for himself and began drinking with his friends in the evenings. It only took a month this time for him to find he was drinking no longer for pleasure but to avoid withdrawal symptoms. He was greatly surprised at how difficult it sometimes was for him to limit his daily intake. Yet he still believed that 'this time' he would manage. Andrew had to slip a long way down, losing his job, wife and family before he was convinced that he could not be a 'social drinker'.

6

Overcoming worry, tension and depression

This chapter is to remind you to apply what you probably already know. Every suggestion made is simple, tried, and known to be effective. Some are comments made by people who themselves suffered with nervousness or depression and who overcame this. Here are some basic guidelines you may find helpful if you are someone who worries over the least thing, getting tensed up, so that you wish everything and everybody would go away ... or that you could just get to sleep and be at peace for a few hours, or if you are someone who worries about the future, or keeps churning over past regrets so that you feel miserable and can't snap out of it.

KEEP BUSY

If your mind is on a task, it cannot also be worrying about something else: 'The secret of being miserable is to have the leisure to bother about whether you are happy or not.'

Physical work or exercise helps. Use your muscles more and your brain less – your brain is fatigued because you are emotionally drained. Physical exercise increases the amount of the body's endorphins, substances that recent discoveries show are likely to be important in feeling well.

Being with other people is another way of keeping busy – people can be your outside interest.

ACCEPT WHAT HAS HAPPENED

No good can come of regrets. Stop yourself as soon as you hear yourself saying 'If only ... if only ...' Brooding over regrets wastes time and valuable emotional energy. Worrying is like a rocking horse – something to do but it doesn't get you anywhere. The only point in occasionally reminding yourself of past failures or stupidity is to give yourself the strength to keep on towards your new goal.

Accepting also means not fighting what must be. If you can no longer drink alcohol safely, accept it. The ancient jujitsu masters taught that a foe could be vanquished by taking the blow and bending with it. Eventually, the foe exhausts himself. But if you struggle to resist when the odds are stacked against you, you risk exhaustion too. Many people who are not religious have found helpful the good sense in Reinhold Nieburhr's prayer (well known to members of Alcoholics Anonymous):

> God grant me the serenity
> To accept the things I cannot change;
> The courage to change the things I can;
> And the wisdom to know the difference.

Accepting means making the most of what you have. You may have lost something that you feel your happiness depended on. But you have not lost everything. Or you may feel life gave you very little. The wise man says 'What can I learn from this misfortune? ... If life gives me a lemon, then I'll make lemonade.' *It may seem over-optimistic to think a disadvantage can be turned on its head; but a crisis in life is a chance for change.* If the most is made of an opportunity for change, a new future may open up. Even if on the first attempt little progress is made, there is the satisfaction of having tried: negative thoughts are replaced by positive thoughts. *Take a risk; try something new.*

SURVIVING MISTAKES

Things go wrong in everyone's lives. 'Survivors' are people who are able to cut their losses, who get out while there is still time and shift their attention to the present and the future instead of dwelling on the past: 'This is the best I could do under the circumstances. Naturally there have been some things wrong, but it does not mean that everything I do is no

'Surviving mistakes'

good.' Two trains of thought to avoid: placing all the blame on others, or going beyond the facts and saying 'What I did was bad, therefore everything I do is bad.'

If your mistakes make you feel ashamed or embarrassed, take care you are not worrying about what idle gossipers are saying. Listen to what your true friends say; take the encouragement they offer.

Look at the 80–90 per cent successful or positive aspects of your life instead of focusing on the 10–20 per cent negative.

Problems and criticism

Worrying can paralyse and can cause procrastination. Dealing with each problem as it comes, chipping away a little at a time, is obviously the best strategy. Making a list of outstanding things to do could be a first step. Don't put it off by taking a drink! Your list may consist of jobs in the house, unpaid bills, tasks at work not done, unopened letters. You can only tackle one thing at a time, but give yourself a designated time for it now. Make yourself too important to heap extra anxiety on yourself. If you are afraid of what you'll find, facing it and doing it is the only way out of that fear.

Handling criticism

Dale Carnegie in *How to Stop Worrying and Start Living** tells how Einstein used to say he was wrong 99 per cent of the time. So he advises that when your anger is rising because you feel you have been unjustly criticised, why not stop and say: 'Just a minute. Einstein said he was wrong 99 per cent of the time. If that's true, maybe I am wrong at least 80 per cent of the time.

---

* *How to Stop Worrying and Start Living* by Dale Carnegie, Cedar Books, 1948, still in print.

Maybe I deserve this criticism. If I do, I ought to be thankful for it – perhaps I can profit by it.' The wise man is prepared to consider he may have made mistakes and learns from them.

Of course, that is the ideal. We all dislike criticism and tend to leap to the defensive: we are not cold logical beings. But a bit of cool logic can help us not to burn up with pointless resentment. If the criticism really is not correct, others have the right to their opinions too. You can agree to disagree.

Handling irritations

Let's not allow ourselves to be upset by small things, things we should scorn and forget, shrug off or allow to pass us by.

SELF-PITY IS DESTRUCTIVE

'People do not understand me.' 'No-one knows what I've been through.' We all have moments when this type of thinking takes over. Some of it may be pride: you may be justly proud that you have withstood so much for so long. But it can be a type of thinking that wastes mental energy. Worse, it may frighten off those who would otherwise help you. So self-pity harms you by burning up precious emotional reserves, and it harms your relationships with those around.

The best cure known to mankind for a bad attack of the 'poor me's' is to think how to give another person some happiness. That may seem difficult, but think about it. Self-pity can keep you stuck like a car in the sand – if you press the accelerator you sink in more deeply.

Sometimes it is helpful to remind yourself that there is always someone worse off than you.

ANGER

It is normal to feel anger. But many people are afraid of, and go to great lengths to avoid, showing it or receiving it. If it gets bottled up then it is in danger of spilling over like a volcano erupting, especially if alcohol has been taken. It can then be out of proportion to whatever triggered it.

It is important to get in touch with feelings of anger. Ask yourself some questions:

1. What situation preceded the feeling?
2. What thought preceded the angry feeling?
3. You can choose to talk yourself into getting more angry. Does it change anything?
4. Can you use your anger to do something positive to change the situation? (Self-assertion: see page 60.)

You can choose to let go of useless anger and talk yourself out of it. This is not the same as pushing it down and suppressing it. Just put it aside and get on with living in the present.

Other people do not 'make' you angry. You are responsible for your own feelings. You may not like what someone has done. You may choose to let it upset you. Or you can choose to tell them calmly, clearly, gently and firmly that you do not like what was done, and explain what would be more acceptable. Then let go.

Attacking the other person verbally or physically just generates more anger. Don't write off a whole person because you have allowed something in their behaviour to upset you. Maybe 80–90 per cent of their behaviour is perfectly acceptable – try to focus on that instead. Talking yourself into getting angry and holding on to that anger harms *you* the most, and deprives you of peace of mind.

SOMEONE TO TALK TO

People may have been saying 'It's all up to you.' As far as the drinking goes, that is 100 per cent correct – it is your responsibility. However, do not feel ashamed if you want to talk to someone about your worries. An injured leg may temporarily need a crutch and so may a stressed mind.

Obviously one should not whine and complain to everyone. Find someone you trust – a relative, a friend, your doctor, minister or priest. You could say something like this: 'May I talk to you? It will help me get my problem into perspective. Perhaps you can give me some advice.' Choose a moment when they will have time or arrange a special time to go back and see them. They will be pleased that you trust them.

There are also agencies where you can talk in confidence to a trained voluntary counsellor. These include the Alcohol Advice Centre or Council on Alcohol, Relate, the Samaritans, a Church counsellor and, for more practical matters, the Citizen's Advice Bureau. Their numbers are in the telephone directory.

Loneliness

People whose marriages have broken down, who have been widowed, or who for some other reason are isolated may feel loneliness acutely. It can be like a physical pain. At first a bereaved person may feel that sustaining a conversation is wearisome. He or she is still numbed by the loss. But at some point, as soon as possible, steps have to be taken to meet people. Meeting new people and making friends is possible for everyone, as long as you do not let yourself be discouraged if your first attempts come to nothing.

Take James for example. He is a technician who lived on his own after his marriage fell apart, partly because of his drinking. He realised, too late for his marriage, that he would have to stop drinking. That was easier to bear than his feelings of loneliness. Being shy, he had never had many friends; but a colleague persuaded him to put a couple of lines in the personal columns of the local newspaper: '40-year old divorced man seeks serious relationship with woman of similar age.' No phone number, just a box number – he was so nervous that an acquaintance might find out and laugh at him. For about the cost of a round of drinks he received 30 serious replies. He contacted three of the correspondents, realising that they were just people like himself. He set out not to bore them with his own worries but to find out about them instead. He discovered that he was a good listener, which pleasantly surprised him. Far from feeling awkward, he found that if he just encouraged the other person to talk about herself, he felt completely at ease. Since he is now happily remarried he says it was the best round he never bought.

Other ways of meeting people are more conventional: evening classes; sports clubs; church; offering your services to a local charity or voluntary organisation. For the over-65s there are lunch-clubs and pensioners' clubs (addresses from local Social Work Department); for the widowed – there is CRUSE, a self-help group, to be found in the telephone directory in larger towns, which provides advice, counselling and opportunities for meeting people informally. The personal columns of the local paper will have details of 'single clubs' and dating agencies.

OVERCOMING NERVOUSNESS

The nervous system has a way of preparing us for action. When there is the need for a sudden burst of energy, for example when danger threatens or we suddenly see the last bus about to leave, blood is diverted from the skin and abdomen to the muscles. The heart beats faster and more strongly. Muscles tighten and their balance is finely set. These reactions would be useful if hunting a dangerous animal but can be annoying, for example, for some people when they go into an interview or enter a room full of people. Most people have experienced anxiety in such situations, but two factors can make anxiety into a nightmare: self-consciousness and the vicious circle.

The individual who is *self-conscious* thinks that the physical changes he or she experiences when nervous, be it tremor, blushing or perspiration, are glaringly obvious to everybody and that everybody who notices them is saying, 'My, that's a nervous person!'

As often as not, no-one notices anything. We know how a tiny hole in one of our teeth seems enormous to us until we actually look at it. The same applies to nervous symptoms. Other people pay little attention to them – they are interested in what we have to say and whether we appear interested in *them*.

If we get anxious because we feel the sensations of anxiety, it's a *vicious circle*. Anxiety then plagues us and we start avoiding a whole range of situations. If you are like this you should develop a relaxation method (see page 39). Above all, as Dr Claire Weekes states in her very useful books,* do not fight it. Struggling against the symptoms can cause more tension, makes more adrenalin flow. Instead, 'float' past your symptoms. Switch into top gear and glide over them. Your anxiety will subside once you have mastered this technique. It needs practice.

Anxiety causes symptoms that may be alarming. The feeling

---

* *Peace from Nervous Suffering* and *Self Help for Your Nerves* by Dr Claire Weekes, Angus & Robertson. 30 years old and still in print!

of the heart bumping or fluttering makes some people fear heart disease. The light-headed dizzy sensation makes people fear they will pass out. This is only a fear – fainting is *very* rare in anxiety unless breathing is allowed to become excessively rapid and shallow and even then recovery is instant. A momentary blankness in our thoughts sometimes makes people fear there is something mentally wrong with them. All these fears are out of proportion. The symptoms are due to anxiety and ALWAYS pass of their own accord. Do not fight them. No-one dies of anxiety. No-one ever went crazy through anxiety.

If you are going through a bad spell with frequent anxiety even several weeks after stopping drinking, do not despair. It will pass. Accept that it may take time. Every journey of a thousand miles begins with a single step.

DEPRESSION WILL PASS

Think of depression as a form of fatigue – emotional draining. It always passes. The term depression has a rather final ring to it. Think instead of a car engine with a flat battery. The battery needs some time and perhaps some recharging and the engine will start again.

Very occasionally, chemical changes have taken place. If so, then the natural recovery process can be speeded up with medication (see page 107). However, most depressions lift in a matter of days or at most a week or two.

First, do not get too worried or fearful about your state. That only makes more demands on already tired emotions.

Second, apply what has already been said about surviving hurt, failure, criticism.

Third, instead of thinking anxiously about yourself do something kind for someone else that will make him or her feel good. Though we cannot change our emotions simply by deciding to, we can change our actions. When we change our actions, our feelings change too. We feel less depressed and miserable while we smile and converse pleasantly with another person. That other person could be the newspaper seller, a colleague, a neighbour, a partner, or the person next in line at the supermarket checkout.

NEGATIVE THINKING

Thoughts can distort our view of reality. Some of the time our thinking functions on auto-pilot. The automatic reactions to guard against are automatic negative thoughts, which can cause depression, feelings of inadequacy, fear, and tension. Here are some common examples:

Looking on the dark side

Dark-side thinkers remember only the 10–20 per cent of what went wrong (on a holiday, for example, or in a job interview) and ignore the 80–90 per cent that went well. Or we see only the flaws in ourselves or someone else, rather than the good qualities.

A cynic converts the positive into the negative and creates a dark place to live in with thoughts such as: 'I got promoted at work, but that just shows what a useless, futile organisation I work for, so what's the point of it all?'

Black and white thinking

This means thinking in extremes, all or nothing. 'I am a total success, or a total failure.' We lose sight of the many shades of grey in between. But no situation is completely black or white, and no-one is totally successful or a total loser. Try not to write off a whole person just because he or she has made a mistake. That includes yourself.

Setting unrealistic goals or living by fixed rules

Notions of perfection or setting ourselves excessively high expectations set up a concept of failure. Thinking 'I must ... I should ... I have to ...' can lead to guilt or disappointment or feelings of failing if you do not achieve all that you set yourself. Be more tolerant of yourself and others. Let go more instead of trying to control more. Be more forgiving. Say 'I should like to ...' or 'I prefer to ...' rather than the tyrannical 'musts' and 'oughts'.

'Here we go again' thinking

This brings history into a new event and distorts it. Just because the last time something like this happened things went wrong, or because a person behaved badly once, it does not mean it will always happen that way. Take each new moment with an open mind. Use your past experience to maximise success, not to predict the future. You never step twice into the same river.

Magnifying unpleasantness

If we magnify the importance of an error or a bit of unpleasant behaviour, we lose sight of the whole issue or event. Take Mary, who argued herself into buying a bottle of wine and drinking it because it was their daughter's birthday and Ian phoned to say he was held up at work. It is true that Mary had made a special meal. But she let herself ignore Ian's flowers that morning, and the way that in recent weeks as a couple they had persevered with her drinking problem and depression.

Was Ian's being late really such a disaster and deliberate hurt, as Mary let herself believe? She should have asked herself: 'Right, now what am I thinking? Am I magnifying the problem?'

Whatever goes wrong for me goes wrong in a big way

Making a catastrophe out of a problem means letting the pendulum swing into the disaster end of the scale. A headache becomes a brain tumour, someone being late becomes a traffic accident. Look out for this kind of thinking and challenge it. Because something is possible does not mean it is probable. We must avoid stirring up anxiety unnecessarily. When a real problem occurs, deal with it then.

Personalising or automatically blaming yourself

If someone is in a bad mood, do you see yourself as being to blame? Beware assuming that others are simply reacting to you; they may not even be thinking of you. Check before making assumptions. Others have their own problems and you are not responsible for how they feel or react.

Jumping to negative conclusions

Sometimes, with little or no evidence, we automatically think that people are thinking the worst of us. We may even react defensively or aggressively to someone before he or she says or does anything. Then we are in danger of talking ourselves out of friends and out of potentially enjoyable occasions. Don't behave like a mind-reader. We cannot know what other people are thinking or feeling until they tell us. Check out assumptions: do things rather than avoid doing them. That will build your confidence. Stop worrying about what others think, instead do what will leave you feeling better.

If you fear that some people will look down on you or spurn you because they may have seen you intoxicated, or heard about your problem, there is only one way to find out. Start seeing them again. They may not have liked your drinking, but it does not mean they have dismissed you as a person.

Feelings are not facts

'I feel helpless, therefore I am helpless.' To *feel* helpless, un-interesting, inadequate etc does not mean you *are* any of these things. Measure the feeling against reality. You can feel very competent and attractive one day, and dull and uninteresting the next. But you are still the same person; nothing but your feelings has changed. Stick with the facts.

Think well and feel great

To do this, you need to challenge faulty thinking. If you detect negative thoughts as we have described here, turn over the coin and consciously focus on the positive aspects, to get a balanced view. If we think more positively, our experience of life is happier.

DEPENDING ON OTHERS FOR APPROVAL

Do you like and value yourself? Or do you depend on others for approval? Letting other people's opinions of you matter more than your own leaves you vulnerable. You may even become a victim of other people and their problems.

As children we depended on our parents for approval and love. We may have learnt to doubt the validity of our own thoughts and feelings and hence ourselves. (This can happen if there is tension in the family, perhaps due to alcohol or to an emotional problem in a parent.) As adults we should not need the approval of others. If we get it, it's a bonus.

If you need approval but get disapproval it can be devastating – a feeling which some people try to anaesthetise with alcohol. It needs practice to wean yourself away from approval-seeking and trying to please others at the expense of yourself. As Mark Twain said, a habit cannot be just thrown out of the window, it needs to be coaxed downstairs a step at a time. Here are tips on beginning that process, on stopping being a victim and taking control of your life:

Valuing yourself

A healthy picture of yourself comes from accepting without complaint your faults and strengths. If you stop putting yourself down and value yourself properly, both your faults and your qualities, you will not need others to make you feel good, nor will you let others make you feel bad. This assessment will give you peace of mind and you will find you can give affection more easily to others. Who are the people you admire and who are good at living? Are they self-destructive? They are bound to have some faults, but do they put themselves down? Do they hide away?

Our guess is that you would probably have no difficulty in writing a list of aspects of yourself which you don't like. Try instead to write a list of what you *do* like about yourself, including those qualities of which you only have a little. For example, you may not be patient all or most of the time – perhaps you would only score 10–20 per cent for patience. But you do have some of that quality, so include it. Do you have some of these qualities: tolerance; imagination; resourcefulness; sense of humour; skill at driving; ability to keep a garden; cooking skills; playing various sports well; ability to appreciate music or films? Write your list in sentences, for example:

- I am good at listening to people
- I am considerate
- I am helpful
- I am good at repairs in the house
- I can make friends easily

Define in detail the skills and attributes you use in your different roles, e.g. as parent, son, daughter, friend, work colleague, leisure group, and not forgetting 'being you' (enjoying a beautiful view, appreciating a debate on TV and so on). Read your list daily and keep adding to it.

What about flaws? We are all imperfect. Some flaws can be altered with guidance and hard work. Others should be accepted, but without letting self-criticism prevent you from enjoying life. Accept, too, that others have faults and stop judging them as well as yourself.

SPEAKING UP FOR YOURSELF

Once you start valuing and respecting yourself more, you will find that others respect you more. Read the Bill of Rights, drawn up by an American family therapist, Virginia Satir (see Figure 7). How many of these rights do you claim for yourself? Work at establishing them. Remember that with rights come responsibilities, for example, not to hurt, attack, or trample on others while achieving these rights. Recognise that other people have these rights too.

You may have used alcohol to feel you are asserting yourself. It is not a help. Alcohol clouds your judgment, distorts your thinking, dulls your perception of others and exaggerates your emotions. What you are saying will be dismissed as the drink talking.

1. I do not have to feel guilty just because someone else does not like what I do, say, think or feel.
2. It is OK for me to feel angry and to express it in responsible ways.
3. I do not have to assume full responsibility for making decisions, particularly where others share responsibility for making the decisions.
4. I have the right to say 'I don't understand' without feeling stupid or guilty.
5. I have the right to say 'I don't know.'
6. I have the right to say NO without feeling guilty.
7. I do not have to apologise or give reasons when I say NO.
8. I have the right to ask others to do things for me.
9. I have the right to refuse requests which others make of me.
10. I have the right to tell others when I think they are manipulating, conning, or treating me unfairly.
11. I have the right to refuse additional responsibilities without feeling guilty.
12. I have the right to tell others when their behaviour annoys me.
13. I do not have to compromise my personal integrity.
14. I have the right to make mistakes and to be responsible for them. I have the right to be wrong.
15. I do not have to be liked, admired or respected by everyone for everything I do.

Figure 7   Bill of Rights, by Virginia Satir.

Some guidelines on constructive self-assertion

- Be open, direct and use 'I', e.g. 'I would like ... I feel ...' 'No, I do not wish to ...'
- Speak calmly, clearly, concisely, but firmly. You don't have to shout to be heard. Just think how carefully people have to listen when someone whispers!
- To be really heard, keep repeating what you have to say again and again like a record needle stuck in a groove. It really works, better than raising your voice.
- You can tell someone you feel angry about something they've done: 'When you do that I feel angry. I would prefer it if you did A,B,C instead.' Let them know positively how they can improve the situation – they may not have any idea how they could do it differently.
- People will only know how you feel or what you want if

'This one's to help me unwind from the office ... this one's to help me wind up to face the wife and kids ... this one's to help me unwind after'.

you put it into words. Expecting people to read your mind is avoiding your responsibility for speaking up for yourself. You can help them respond more positively, rather than having to guess and getting it wrong.

- If you are trying to get someone to change something, gather your facts, and have specific examples of what is wrong.
- Pick a time when the person you are going to speak to is not otherwise occupied and you will not be interrupted.
- Stay on target, sticking to what is important.
- If you feel anger building up, talk yourself down ('I'm not going to burn up any more of my precious emotional energy than is absolutely necessary!').

- Don't insist on winning every single point, just the important ones.

The more you speak up for yourself, the better you will be heard and the stronger you will feel. Don't let the drink do the talking!

COPING WITH SLEEPLESSNESS

People vary in how much sleep suits them. Some people are happy with four hours a night, others with seven or eight. The older you are the less sleep you need. Alcohol can make you go to sleep sooner than you might otherwise, but often causes an unpleasant wakefulness at 2 or 3 a.m. This is a 'rebound' effect (see page 15). Sleeping tablets usually do not have this rebound effect, partly because the drug is still in the blood in the morning – this is why they cause a hangover in some people. Both alcohol or sleeping tablets, if taken regularly at night for a month or more, suppress the normal function of the brain's sleep centre. This gradually recovers over three or four weeks if sleeping tablets or 'nightcaps' are stopped. But during the recovery period it will at first be impossible to get off to sleep at the usual time and you dream more than usual. Eventually sleep will go back to a normal pattern.

Sleeping tablets are best avoided except for periods of less than three weeks and it is wise to take them on alternate nights only. Apart from long use of sleeping tablets or alcohol, the commonest cause of the feeling that sleep is poor is the belief that a magic seven or eight hours a night is necessary. If this belief is held by someone who has little to look forward to in the coming day, it can lead to excessive worrying about sleep. Then an effort is made to get to sleep earlier and earlier, but the sleep centre cannot be willed. It has its own rhythm. The more a person worries about not sleeping the more tense he or she becomes. No-one can sleep if they are tense.

Worry is also a cause of sleeplessness. Sleep does not come if the mind is overactive and preventing the body from relaxing. At night a tired nervous system can trick you into thinking that your problems cannot be beaten. Don't be tricked. Make a list of your problems on a piece of paper and leave it till the morning when your mind is fresh. On page 35 we made simple suggestions about encouraging sleep, such as going to bed late, relaxing in a warm bath, reading, having a bedtime snack or warm milk drink (but avoid tea and coffee after 6 p.m.). Physical tiredness helps, so take more exercise.

When you go to bed just lie still. Don't try to sleep. You can't make yourself sleep. But if you have learnt to relax (see page 39) you can drift off more easily. Self-hypnosis cassette tapes from bookshops work for many people. As long as you lie still with your muscles relaxed you know your body is getting rest.

If you are just too tense, get up and do something. Don't lie there worrying. Above all do not worry about not sleeping – lack of sleep will not seriously harm you.

THE SECRETS OF WELL-BEING

How do people successfully come through a crisis in their lives? Successful people have not been spared set-backs, but they see these as positive experiences – opportunities for change. They rarely feel cheated or disappointed by life. They are cheerful people who have friends and who work at keeping up friendships.

They are not thin-skinned or sensitive to criticism. Survivors are people who have learnt to distinguish between the qualities and abilities of their underlying self and, on the other hand, the value they have in a given situation: they know they cannot be expert in everything!

Survivors do not see an attack on their work or ideas as an attack on their real value as a person, and so neither react with uncontrolled anger or defensiveness, nor absorb the blow so that it erupts later, for example as depression or grumbling resentment. Survivors can also distinguish between what is their problem and what is someone else's problem.

7

For women

In this book, we often say 'he' rather than 'she'. But nowadays, with more shops and supermarkets selling alcohol, massive advertising campaigns trying to show alcoholic drinks as glamorous and liberating for women, and more cultural expectations that women will drink, the number of women with a serious alcohol problem has increased. Today, there is almost one woman with a serious alcohol problem for every two men.

HOW ARE WOMEN AFFECTED?

If the mother is the backbone of a family, the family knows when drinking affects her emotions, causing her to be irritable or tired. But she may have been trying for months or years to cover up her drinking. Perhaps she drinks in secret, keeping bottles in drawers or cupboards. If she has had too much to drink she will claim 'flu and got to bed. Embarrassment perhaps leads to her hiding the empties and disposing of them secretly; or she goes through this palaver because she has begun to get annoyed at her husband checking up on her. She may buy her drink in different places so that no-one will know how much she gets through. The sheer effort of covering up can eventually take any pleasure out of drinking.

Is it pleasurable? Yes, some who are heading for a problem have been through a phase where they believe they are wittier or more charming with a drink, so having a drink has become essential before socialising. A drink becomes a reward for a hard day at work, or for a boring day of household chores. Perhaps it began as a treat which helped fill the gap after the children left home and the nest was empty. Or it may have been a temporary way of switching off from worry, frustration or hurt. But that's the kind of drinking that starts a habit. When stress comes, and alcohol is used 'to help cope' with it, that's dangerous. Have you used alcohol in these ways?

How are your friends and relatives reacting when you drink? Have you been the worse for drink at social outings or parties? Have you phoned people up, late at night, after you are well topped up, with rambling conversations or repetitive tales of woe? You may even get a bit hazy about some of those evenings when you were at home drinking, and not recall whom you phoned. Now you can see that you may be putting some friendships under strain; or why you are perhaps even losing some friends!

STAYING OFF DRINK

If you have decided to make a No Alcohol rule for yourself, give yourself the chance to succeed. Beware of saying that since you've decided to stop for ever, one drink today will not matter, that you will stop tomorrow. Start today, and take it one day at a time.

Do I need to know why I drink?

Diabetics do not need to know why they developed diabetes; they simply know that there is a regime they must follow each day to stay well. Do not expend energy in going over what caused you to drink to excess. Whatever factors were involved to start with may not be so important now anyway – the drinking can take on a life of its own. Just concentrate, one day at a time, on staying away from that first drink. Keeping strong and well is important.

To stay off drink, you need to feel strong and well

Eat a balanced diet. Your body may be short of vitamins. Vitamin B supplements, obtainable from the chemist's, are advisable. If you have been prone to premenstrual tension (PMT), then you may want to take evening primrose oil with Vitamin E, and B6 in the two weeks before your period. Those of our patients who are prone to premenstrual blues find that, if they relapse into drinking again, it is most likely to happen in the week before their period starts.

Take extra exercise, beginning slowly without pushing yourself. Muscles may have been severely weakened by the alcohol intake of years and will take a month or two to recover. Exercise also has a good effect on the brain and helps your sense of well-being.

If you are in your late 40s or 50s and your periods are heavy or irregular, or you have begun to experience flushing and sweating, hormone replacement therapy (HRT) can be helpful and nowadays it is proven to be safe. It must be prescribed by your doctor. Do not mistake sweating, shakiness, panicky feelings, tiredness or depression for the menopause if you are still drinking. Alcohol can cause all these symptoms.

What emotions might undermine my strength?

Do you have a feeling of being taken for granted? A great deal is expected of women, and some do not recognise that they have just slipped into doing it all – until resentment builds up. Have you gradually done more and more for your partner, or the children, or at work, and begun to feel angry that your efforts go unnoticed? Have you been expected to look after an elderly relative? Rewarding though that can sometimes be, have you let yourself be worn down by the demands, and perhaps let resentment build up that brothers or sisters are not doing their share?

Here are some guidelines:

1. You have a right to set limits to what is expected of you.
2. You do not have to feel guilty if you say 'No'. You may think that, because of your drinking, you have lost all your credit, your right to say what you want, what you think, what you feel. If you think this, you are wrong. Some people in the family, or at work, may seem to believe that, but their main wish is for you to succeed at stopping drinking, and now you are taking steps to do that. You are not blaming them for your drinking; the drinking was your responsibility. But you can ask for the conditions that may help you along the road to staying sober.
3. You do not have to let anger build up inside. What is the point of letting that happen anyhow? Carrying anger and resentments is the last thing you need now.
4. Avoid 'if only' thinking about the past: 'If only I had not said that ... If only we had not moved house.' The past cannot be changed, only accepted and learnt from.

Give yourself space

You may not be used to having time for you. All your time has been occupied by housework, maybe a paid job, and then perhaps being at the beck and call of your partner or children. Now that you are getting well, if you are at home all day you may find you are getting everything done by 11 a.m. There may be an unexpected emptiness, a feeling of 'What next?' You may have lost the knack of how to make the most of time for yourself. Make it a part of your new regime to take up some activity. This could mean reviving a hobby or interest from the past, or just calling on a friend. Or something completely new? Why not make a list of what you would like to do for yourself?

Recharging your batteries

As well as setting some limits to what is asked of you, and saving some of your emotional energy, your emotional batteries may need some new input, some stimulation. This applies especially if because of divorce or bereavement you are now alone. It applies too if you do not have a paid job but your husband is at that point in his career where he is in great demand, taken up with work, not putting time aside to do things with you, or away from home a lot.

- If you renew contact with friends, join a class, or take on a part-time job, or in another way make something of a new life for yourself, that will actually make you feel happier.
- Do not resent your partner having his interests and friends. Couples often function best if each has his and her own outside interests that you can talk about together as long as there are still some things you do together.
- It is not easy for someone whose confidence has been damaged to make new starts. Crossing the hurdle means taking a risk, a risk that you will find the class you apply for uninteresting; or that a friend you get back in touch

with to go to a yoga or dance class may be too busy that day. Usually friends like very much to be asked to help, because that is what friendship is about. They may welcome you taking the initiative because they have been too diffident to do so themselves. Don't be misled by outward appearances of confidence in a friend, she may be just as lacking in confidence as you.

YOUR PARTNER'S ATTITUDE

Will your partner and you get on better when you stop drinking? He's probably going to be proud and pleased you are doing something about it. But as you realise, all may not instantly be rosy. Getting him to start taking notice of your views and opinions again may cause friction: change can be difficult for him too. Till recently you may have felt your drinking disqualified you from making decisions in the relationship. Or your partner may have increasingly grown to ignore your views, out of anger or because he has lost trust in your reliability.

- Give him time to get used to the new 'you'.
- When he responds sensitively to your needs, react positively to let him know how much that means to you.
- If you are putting your views across more forcefully now that you have stopped drinking, this may be new for him. You both need re-educating in teamwork – for example, in dealing with the children or in deciding how to spend your time.
- Listen, without interrupting defensively, if he wants to tell you what he is thinking and feeling.

Feeling steam-rollered?

Did you used to feel he steam-rollered you sometimes, over-ruled your views, or did not even ask your opinion? If so, be careful you do not go on harbouring resentments about that.

Your partner may have had to take over extra responsibilities at home if alcohol affected your competence, or made you unreliable or over-reactive. On the other hand, he too may well have been out of control sometimes, in his frustration and anger with you! You do not have to condone that, but try to understand how he might have felt. It is up to you to start getting the balance in the relationship right, and if you are not drinking you will make headway.

If you feel he has taken over, or is trying to control you, do not assert your rights by drinking again, perhaps showing him that you are an independent agent by drinking where and what you like. You will just regret it later as you go through the old cycle of drinking, hassle, remorse, feeling you have failed, asserting 'your right to drink' … and so round and round in a circle that can go on for years.

If you are sober, you can chip away at showing your partner that you too have views and wishes and are responsible enough to follow through on what needs to be done for the two of you. Being appropriately assertive does not mean being aggressive. But you have rights too (see page 61).

What if my partner drinks heavily?

Where there is a woman with an alcohol problem there is often a heavy-drinking man in her life, the commonest such figure being either father or partner (or, less often, a work colleague). If a parent used alcohol as a drug to change mood (it is our favourite drug after all), a daughter will often pick that up at a young age. In later life, women sometimes slip into heavy drinking just to join in with a husband or boyfriend who drinks. 'If you can't beat them, join them.' 'At least now we go out for a drink together, while before I hardly ever saw him.' This type of thinking can lead to disaster. What may start as fun drinking together can, if the drinking of either of you gets out of control, result in some nasty moments.

Drinking to help cope with a partner's drunken behaviour may at first dull the annoyance and disgust you feel at it, but it can end in serious dependence on alcohol and a worse problem than your partner's.

Bridging the gap

Your partner may have become cold and distant during your drinking. He may not see that he should start thinking about how he is reacting and about what he can do to help, rather than just handing you over to a clinic and expecting you to get 'cured'.

Let him know that it will mean a lot to you if he can support you and discuss what you feel about the relationship. But also let him know that you take full responsibility for the drinking and that you are doing something about it.

8

Your choice – teenagers and drinking

Many teenagers have an evening when they drink too much. Alcohol is a drug which takes time to get used to. You vomit or you have a hangover, or your head does not work at school or college next day. A few teenage drinkers pass out and end up in hospital, or are crazy enough to drive a car in that state. Not many will go on repeating this behaviour. *But if you keep on getting into trouble because of your drinking and you do not or cannot cut back, you're developing an alcohol problem.*

Some young people decide they cannot predictably control their drinking once they have had one or two drinks. So they give alcohol up. You meet some very young people at Alcoholics Anonymous these days, who seem really pleased at their decision.

Others will want to make a new start with alcohol, and practise drinking sensibly. You have to work at it, though, especially if you are someone who likes getting high on alcohol – because, in that case, not going over a sensible dose of alcohol can be tricky.

WHY SHOULDN'T I DRINK WHEN I'M FED UP?

It's your choice. But does drink really help? Alcohol can switch off the brain, but it can make depression much worse. Also, we can say or do things we later regret if we have had that much alcohol. Sharing what you feel with someone else, and doing that before you drink, is a better way of getting out of the blues. Sometimes you get good advice by talking to someone else. It can also help you see more clearly what you really do feel, what you want and what you can do to put things right. Sometimes you realise you have let things seem worse than they really are – most people get the poor-me's now and again (see chapter 6). If you cannot discuss your problem or your feelings with a parent, speak to one of your friends, a friend's parent, another of your relatives, a counsellor at your school or college, or the personnel officer at work.

HOW ELSE CAN I FEEL RELAXED AT A PARTY?

Do you think you are shy? So what! Shy people are often extremely kind, good people to know; they can be sensitive and interesting. You may think you look nervous, but probably others do not notice it and it does not matter anyhow.

Maybe you would like to know what to say when you are out with people. Your best approach is to ask other people something about themselves: 'How are you enjoying the party?' or 'Hi, I'm Jackie, how do you like this kind of music?' Basically other people like to talk about themselves. You can be a good listener – show your interest by attending carefully to what is said, nod, smile, and draw your companion out by getting them to elaborate more on what they say. You'll come across as charming. Your shyness will vanish if you stop thinking about what other people think of you, and show a genuine interest in others instead.

HOW CAN I STOP GOING OVER THE TOP WITH MY DRINKING?

You will have to set yourself a limit on how much you will drink on any particular occasion. Remember that:

- A glass of wine = 1 unit
- Half a pint of ordinary strength beer, lager or cider = 1 unit
- Some cans or bottles of strong lager = 3 units
- Half a bottle of vodka = 15 units
- A glass of 1 per cent lager – one-third unit
- A glass of Coca-Cola – 0 units

You will be safe if you stay at or below three units during a party, evening out or whatever. Above that level you will begin to look drunk and you will be less able to control what you drink next. Avoid all spirits and strong lagers. It is easier to control your intake by drinking shandy (lemonade plus beer or lager) or ordinary (3 per cent) lagers. Best of all, space your alcoholic drinks with soft drinks or take low alcohol lager.

One drink takes 30 minutes to have its maximum effect on the brain. It will be active for one hour. Space your drinks! Eat some food!

Saying No

Say 'No' if you do not want an alcoholic drink. You do not need to give a reason for this. Keeping your head and not giving way to pressure shows you have personality. Remember, you have a *right* to say 'No'.

ADVICE TO PARENTS

- Explain the facts about alcohol and about the different drinks available.
- Introduce sensible drinking at home if your teenager asks for a drink.
- Advise food to reduce the chance of getting drunk.
- Inform about the law – in most countries the minimum age for buying alcohol is 18.
- No drinking when driving, cycling or swimming.
- What example are you setting? Young people learn more from what you do than from what you say.

9

How is the family affected?

WHEN THE DEFENCES GO UP

The family of someone with a drinking problem may suffer for years without recognition or help. The changes in the family are often gradual and at first are hard to understand. Tensions begin to build up. Perhaps the person who is drinking is erecting a defensive wall around himself or herself. This wall is to protect them from comment or criticism. It is also to protect the drinking, which is becoming more necessary, especially if he or she is experiencing withdrawal symptoms without alcohol. The more guilt he or she feels about the consequences of the drinking, the more touchy is the response to criticism, real or merely expected. This protective wall becomes harder to penetrate. Members of the family in turn put up their own defences to avoid feeling hurt or neglected. Each person in the family becomes more isolated and the drinker becomes less and less sensitive to the real needs and attitudes of family and friends, and how they may be suffering.

STRESS: UNCERTAINTY, GUILT, HURT

Some of the causes of stress in the family are more obvious than others – for example, if there are financial worries or if the drinker has to face trouble at work or a court appearance.

Other stresses are less easy for outsiders to understand. There is the UNCERTAINTY and unpredictability for the family if one member has a drinking problem. Will she be all right at tea-time today, or will she be the worse for drink and bad-tempered? Will he be home on time tonight, or will I have to wait for hours not knowing when and in what state he'll return? It is very hard to plan ahead. You cannot plan meals or outings. Family life becomes highly unpredictable.

Many relatives go through a period where they feel a vague GUILT for not doing more to prevent episodes of excessive drinking. Even last resorts fail – going drinking with him in an effort to control his drinking, or pouring the drink away. If you are someone who lacks confidence, the pressures when your partner, child, parent or friend has a drinking problem can reduce your confidence further. The blame for things going wrong may be laid at your door. You may even be blamed for the drinking. All manner of criticisms and accusations are hurled at you in moments of anger, and you may be made to feel you have failed. You may believe that outsiders blame you too.

A partner may find herself in a position where she 'cannot do the right thing'. She can begin to feel a failure as a wife, a mother and a person. She feels her only contacts with her husband are when he wants food, sex or some kind of help. Many of the HURTS are very difficult to discuss: the aggress-iveness, perhaps the bed-wetting (not uncommon in people who consume very large amounts of alcohol), the revulsion she may be beginning to feel about sexual contact.

She may feel extremely angry, but finds her angry outbursts

when her partner has been drinking are pointless or even lead to him turning on her.

THE STRAIN OF COVERING UP

The wives of problem drinkers are often treated by their doctor for stress symptoms – 'nerves', depression, backache, exhaustion – without revealing the real cause of their distress. The wife returns home clutching tranquillizers or a tonic because she wishes to cover up and protect her husband and herself from the shame and humiliation she imagines might result if the problem is revealed. In this way neither gets the help they really need – the agony is prolonged instead of faced. The longer the cover-up continues, the longer the drinking continues. Ask yourself if you are making the drinking *more* possible by this type of behaviour.

PRACTICAL FAMILY MATTERS

If it is the husband who has the drinking problem, his wife sometimes has to take over some of the tasks he may have been responsible for – paying bills, disciplining the children, making decisions concerning the home. Drinking is expensive and in some families money cannot be found for the bills, let alone for the children's school outings or new clothes. Some wives resort to taking money out of their husbands' pockets at night for the next day's necessities.

If it is the wife who is spending money on drinking the husband may find himself trying to control every penny in a desperate attempt to prevent his wife being under the influence of alcohol when the children are around. If it is she who has the responsibility for the home, and he who has a full-time job, he may end-up becoming completely responsible for the house-keeping, perhaps even stopping her getting credit at local shops – which makes her feel humiliated and angry.

HOW ARE THE CHILDREN AFFECTED?

Parents often say 'the children don't really know'. They are usually wrong. Even *young* children are aware if a parent has a drinking problem. Here are some of the ways children are affected:

- One of their parents is now less and less 'available' – as a guide, as a source of love, encouragement, companionship and someone they can trust.
- If their parents are getting on badly, children feel their loyalties divided. Strife between parents causes great distress to children. Older children may try to intervene; younger children withdraw. In such families, the children tend to develop problems – delinquency, aggressiveness (perhaps imitating what they have seen at home) nervousness and fearfulness; bed-wetting; physical complaints, perhaps without any medical basis. The general unhappiness and stress shows up at school too, for example, by falling behind in class or by truancy.
- Children learn by example and are at risk of developing a similar problem later in life (see page 20).
- When a parent's drinking problem has become severe and the other parent is not coping, one of the children may find adult responsibilities thrust on him – mothers sometimes say 'he took his father's place'. Some children find the responsibilities too much, others cope well. Take John for example ... The youngest of three sons, on the surface he seemed to be perfectly stable. He was 14 when his school-teachers asked the family doctor why John's attendance at

school was so poor. His mother was drinking heavily. This always worsened her tendency to depression and her back pain from her slipped disc. She would lie in bed, feeling very sorry for herself. Her husband worked long shifts – 7 a.m. to 7 p.m. John felt he had to stay at home to make sure she was all right. He feared she would become intoxicated and fall; or, as once happened, go to sleep with a cigarette in her hand and burn the bedclothes. He was afraid that if he was at school she would drink more. He lost touch with his friends, stopped going to his clubs and fell behind in class. Outwardly he was the model son. Underneath he felt very resentful. When he was 16 he suddenly and angrily broke off all contact with his parents to go and live with his brother 200 miles away. His mother was deeply hurt at his complete rejection. Then, patiently, she allowed time to pass for him to gain his sense of independence, and to let him and the rest of the family see that she was at last determined to tackle her alcohol problem. But during the two years that elapsed she frequently felt that she had lost him for ever.

SEPARATION AND DIVORCE

Divorce is equally common in families whether it is the wife or the husband who has the drinking problem. Some men have real fears about the care of the children if their partners' role includes childcare more or less full-time, and the wife's drinking has affected day to day living and made her unreliable. Of course, separation or divorce is usually very upsetting for all the family. We know couples where in the end it turned out to be a good solution for all concerned, but we know many more who worked at their marriages and did well.

10

How can I help?

First, if you want to help, let the person know that you are prepared to help and to give support if he or she is ready to make changes. Be prepared to go for help with him or her. Offer reassurance that while you may feel bitter and resentful, you still care about what happens to your partner/relative/friend.

Let the drinker know what you can and can't tolerate. But don't make him/her out to be the 'baddie' and you the 'goodie'. We all have our faults. Let your partner know if you have been feeling miserable, low or lonely, without making it seem like a further attack. Be ready to give appreciation and encouragement, and recognise how rarely you have been doing that lately. Be prepared to look at what you do that makes things worse and to accept criticism.

Be prepared to seek outside support for yourself. This may help you to understand the problem better and to be more effective in bringing about changes. It may be hard to do it alone. Many people really do understand, many have gone through similar difficulties themselves. People care about what happens to you too. Try a meeting of Al-Anon (see page 111). Be prepared to attend a number of meetings; give it a chance – there are no instant solutions. Or talk to someone at a Council on Alcoholism (see page 112).

Avoid protecting the drinker from the consequences of his or her drinking, since that makes it easy for them to continue. Don't make excuses for them anymore.

Recognise that months or years of bitterness and resentment will have left some mark. You will have to put real effort into building a new life together. But isn't this better than putting so much energy into the 'big cover-up'?

Don't waste energy in trying to control the person's drinking. If he or she is determined to drink there is little that another person can do until he or she has a change of mind. You are not responsible for another person's drinking. It is the other person who decides to take that drink. Of course, there may be times when this rule is difficult to put into practice – if you can see a particular situation coming up when to drink would have serious consequences. But it is an important principle which has helped many to free themselves from a frustrating and fruitless struggle.

HOW CAN I GET THROUGH THE DENIAL?

Your partner or relative may minimise the drinking and the problems, perhaps even tell lies. Most of us prefer not to be reminded of our foolish or hurtful mistakes. But for someone with a drinking problem to talk of giving up or reducing drinking may be upsetting in itself – alcohol, or the pub, has become a very important part of life, perhaps even a crutch. He or she may have been using alcohol to dull awareness of worries or other problems.

Confronting this denial needs the right timing. Never try it when he or she has been drinking or is still intoxicated. The 'morning after' may be a good time, or if there is a crisis. Do not always try to keep the peace on the morning after. If that morning he or she is not drinking and feels wretched or

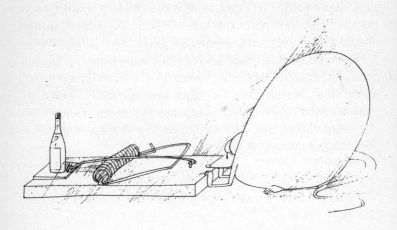

remorseful, use the opportunity to explain the harm that surrounds the drinking, without it seeming to be an attack. Help the drinker to weigh up the pros and cons of his or her drinking and try to persuade him or her to make a firm decision and perhaps to seek outside help. If your relative or friend agrees to seek outside help make the appointment straight away. *Go with them.*

Don't make idle threats. Only make threats if you really mean what you say. Sometimes if a crisis is allowed to occur it may bring about important changes for the better, though it may be distressing at the time.

Though difficult, it may be useful to have a family get-together at a time when your partner has not been drinking. The children's understanding, caring and honesty about how they feel can be a helpful eye-opener. No parent wants their children to be unhappy and hurt by their actions. The drinker may feel the children have turned against him or her. But the children may rarely get a chance to let their parent know that they care greatly. Never try to turn the children against your partner. Children need the love of both parents. Children should stay out of their parents' quarrels.

Try to think of the good and positive things you can all aim for. Think of different ways that you and your partner can spend time more happily, together and separately. Compromises may be necessary – be prepared to do some things that the other likes doing, with the agreement that he or she will join in some things you prefer.

WHAT IF THERE'S NO CHANGE AT ALL?

It may be a long time before your partner is really ready to tackle the problem. Meanwhile you have to survive. Try to help yourself and the children to lead normal lives as much as possible. Don't wait around for the drinker to come home. Put more energy into activities that help you to get some enjoyment out of your life. Detach yourself from your partner's problems. Don't continually make that person's problems yours. And don't churn up with anger – it only harms you.

Decide on some limits, keep to them, and hand your partner back the responsibility for his or her behaviour. You are responsible for what *you* think, feel and do – not for someone else's thoughts, feelings or actions.

You and the children can live your lives until your partner decides to change. But the last thing you need is to harm your self-esteem, which is already being put at risk, by behaving badly in any way that you will later regret.

THE DRINKING'S STOPPED BUT PERHAPS YOU'RE NOT FEELING MUCH HAPPIER

For years you have been saying: 'If only the drinking would stop, everything would be all right.' Now it's stopped but maybe you are still not feeling much better. Perhaps the honeymoon is over. Here are some of the dilemmas you may face:

- Perhaps he or she now wants to take over managing the money again, but you are afraid the improvement will not last. It's hard to trust again.
- Perhaps he or she wants to take over disciplining the children again. You may disagree about how this should be done and the children may rebel against it. Older children will find it hard to let go of the freedom, or the special closeness with you, that they have had recently.
- Perhaps you resent the encouragement going to your partner for stopping drinking, while no-one seems to appreciate all you have had to put up with and the changes you have had to make. It can be puzzling and distressing to feel this way when everyone expects you to be grateful.
- Perhaps memories are still painful. In a marriage where one partner has had a drinking problem, the other partner often takes a long time to forgive and forget, especially if past injuries have left deep wounds.

Alec and Mary, a couple in their 30s, experienced some of these difficulties. Things went well for three or four weeks as Alec was determined to do something about his drinking. But Mary's anger at all the broken promises of that last year was only just below the surface. She criticised his wallpapering when at last he got round to redecorating the lounge. She complained when he brought the boys home late after taking them (for the first time in years) to a football match. Inside she felt bad for getting angry with him when he was doing all that

'. . . at last he got round to redecorating the lounge.'

was asked of him. She was puzzled that she felt annoyed when
their relatives gave Alec pats on the back for doing so well. 'If
only they knew how hard it's been for me,' she used to say to
herself. Alec did not understand her grumpiness – and nearly
reacted by drinking again.

Some wives are baffled at having given their husbands the
first drink again. They found it impossible to tolerate the
atmosphere when he was sober. 'He was getting on my nerves,
always watching me; always restless. I went out and bought
him some beer so that he'd leave me in peace.' A wife may feel
inadequate when her now competent husband is around more
and is now criticising HER. This can, of course, also be true of
husbands whose wives have stopped drinking. Perhaps your
self-confidence needs building up again. Think of something
you can do that will give you a sense of achievement. Your

partner will enjoy having a happier and more confident companion. Ask for your spouse's support in a nice way, not in a crotchety grudging way. He or she may be pleased to be asked.

- Be prepared to accept criticism if it is justified. Some partners have found it hard to be on the receiving end of criticism: 'After all I've had to put up with, how dare she criticise me!' But we all have our faults. Try not to enter into battles about small things. Accept that you may see some matters differently, and that this may be a good thing.

  Don't harbour grudges or anger. Be open and honest about what has upset you without being accusing or attacking: 'Maybe you don't realise that when you do THAT it really upsets me. Maybe there's something I've done that upsets you?'
- Say at least three positive, appreciative things to your partner each day.
- Don't forget Al-Anon meetings (see page 111). Al-Anon has a wealth of experience, understanding and unsentimental advice and helps families develop a more positive attitude to everyday life.

Our next chapter touches on some of the commoner problems in marriage. Some aspects of your relationship may need working on if there are to be real improvements when your partner stops drinking.

A WORD TO TEENAGERS

Life in the family has probably been far from easy for you lately. However, if your parent has decided to begin to do something about his or her drinking problem, you may like some hints about how you can help:

Try to avoid power struggles with your parents. If you tackle them in a reasonable way and not in a grumpy, accusing way they are more likely to be fair in return. If it's an argument about what time you are to come home, explain what you want to do. Obviously, a friendly attitude will get the best results. An affectionate hug of reassurance – he or she may feel very guilty for letting you down in recent months – may be shrugged off with embarrassment but will be greatly appreciated.

Your parent has been suffering and struggling with a problem that may take a great deal of courage and determination to conquer. You should never feel to blame for the drinking, but your care and concern shown in a loving way will be a great help.

COPING WITH SETBACKS

So your partner promised to abstain or greatly reduce the drinking. Be prepared for occasional relapses when drinking may be excessive. Take a positive attitude. Don't be too ready to accuse, but don't pretend it is not happening until it really gets out of hand. Confront him in a direct but caring way, and when he's NOT had a drink. Let her know you still want to work towards improving matters. Let your husband/son know that his drinking or increased drinking is affecting the family. Let your wife/daughter know you are still concerned for her. Set your limits, but try not to make the drinker feel too bad and

$1 \times$ *need not* $=$ $+$

so take refuge in more alcohol. Drinkers who are trying to stop, but make a slip, will probably be feeling pretty bad already about letting themselves and the family down.

Sometimes people have said that they found themselves taking a drink, and knowing there would be such anger on their return home decided they might as well have a real session and 'be hung for a sheep as for a lamb'.

If your relative starts drinking again it may be time to seek outside help. If you have already been having outside help you may fear that you will be turned away this time because things have failed. Don't let that fear put you off renewing contact. Something positive can come out of a relapse – a new understanding of what the real difficulties are. But don't spend too much effort tracing events back if he or she genuinely cannot understand why or how the relapse happened.

Don't say: 'It's a disaster, we're back to square one.' Instead remind your partner how well he or she has done, and what has been achieved so far. You may be angry and disappointed, but don't lose sight of how difficult it may have been for your partner. Check within yourself that you, too, have not given up making the extra effort. It's easy to fall back into old habits. Positive encouragement will lead to more rewarding results than angry carping.

11

For a husband whose wife drinks

The fact that you are reading this book shows that you want to understand someone with an alcohol problem and find new ways of helping. If it is your wife or female partner who drinks, you may be feeling puzzled about why this happens even at the times you would most expect her to be trying not to drink – when you are about to go out to a function or gathering, for example, or when you have friends visiting, or when you feel that you, her husband, have made a particular effort. This can be very disappointing, even frustrating. You may have felt very angry, even despairing.

If you have been trying to control your wife's drinking, you may be in a vicious circle. If she wants to drink, she will. So first, a few 'don'ts'.

DON'TS

Don't waste time on a bottle hunt. If she is still at a stage of alcohol dependence, where she feels alcohol is her lifeline, she will resent this with great anger and simply replenish her supply.

Don't discuss important things if she is intoxicated.

Don't extort promises that she will never drink again. She may promise with sincerity, but if she has already tried to stop several times and failed she may now need help. She may otherwise be building up more failure for herself.

Don't go over her faults and failings, bringing up the past. Don't worsen her feeling of failure by comparing her to others, or slipping into the holier-than-thou role where you are the model husband who selflessly takes on all and leaves his wife with nearly nothing to do, and stops drinking to prove to his wife how easy it is.

Don't do anything to increase the distance between you. She has become hypersensitive to what you say and how you look at her, too ready to see criticism and negative judgment.

Don't become a surveillance expert. If she is trying to stop drinking, she may prefer you not to check up on her. She wants your confidence, for you to recognise her strengths. However, if she has been abstinent and then has a slip, it may be better to speak to her about it sooner rather than later, in case there is something you can do to help her out of the relapse.

STEPS TO TAKE

Learn to see the problem not as a moral failure or as badness. You will then be better able to help her not to see it in that way. Then she will be less racked by guilt and may deny the problem less. Her self-confidence needs rebuilding, not dismantling further. If she can be helped to see that an alcohol problem can develop in strong as well as less strong people, she may stop believing that she is simply weak.

Decide to help her, to care for her. This may mean that she needs to seek other advice as well, be it medical help, counselling, or Alcoholics Anonymous – or to at least read some of this book.

Think about what you can do to enrich your marriage. Arrange to go out together, take an interest in how she dresses, in her hair or make-up and in what interests her. If you ask for advice on how you can help, do not take her comments as criticism and react angrily – we can all improve our marriages. You must really LISTEN to what she has to say.

If your marriage has become a power struggle where one person has to win and the other lose, you may need some outside help. You will have to work at understanding each other, and find a method of solving problems rather than winning points.

Those traditional prerogatives of the wife which, perhaps, you took over when she was drinking – organising the house-hold, making the children's arrangements, making meals – should now begin to be handed back if she is the full-time home-maker. When the drinking has stopped, your wife will be as competent as she was before.

Be positive and encouraging. You can do this without being pompous or paternalistic! Your comments and attitudes are very important to her.

Focus on the 80–90 per cent positive points rather than the 10–20 per cent negative. Say at least three positive, appreciative things to her each day.

12

Marriage and the sexual relationship

All marriages go through bad patches. In some these last for a matter of days, in others weeks may pass before an atmosphere of anger or resentment clears. If nothing is done to work out what is going wrong, grumpiness and tension will soon be back. If you cannot work it out together it may be worth contacting a marriage counsellor. In this chapter we touch on a few of the more common difficulties.

COMMUNICATION

If you are feeling depressed, resentful or dominated because you are not getting what you want from your marriage, ask yourself: 'Does my partner know what I want?' Or have you just assumed that he or she does? Also ask: 'What am I really giving my partner?' Is the giving one-sided or balanced?

Take Dorothy, for example. When she came for marriage counselling, she used to stare at the nearest planet and say things like: 'Some people go on holidays ...' Her expression varied between martyrdom and sarcasm. What she should have said was 'I'd like to go on holiday. Can we discuss whether it will be possible?' Don't assume. Be clear and frank.

'Another marriage on the rocks, dear?'

It is definitely possible to be frank in a kind way, without being accusing or blaming.

Mutual respect is important. If you feel the balance is unfair or you are being taken advantage of, but are too timid to ask for what you want, then remember: no-one respects a doormat.

The other side of this coin is that we have to *listen carefully* to what our partners want because they may have difficulty in putting it clearly. You can be sure, however, that they give clues all the time. They may often want you to be a loyal friend, a source of appreciation, encouragement or comfort.

Be a good listener. It may sometimes be difficult to change how your partner is feeling; but you will find it helps if you listen to how he or she feels. This means not immediately trying to argue or jolly them out of it, or jumping to your own defence. *Listen*!

GIVING TO GET

If you want changes, try to reach an agreement on what you can both do towards an improvement. Keep it simple. If it's your untidiness that annoys your husband, and one of the things that upsets you is his refusal to give you time away from the children, then sign a contract (make a bit of a joke about it) stating that you agree to keep your clothes and the kitchen tidy if he agrees to take the children out on Saturday afternoons. Run the contract for two weeks – or until one of you breaks it! What worked for two weeks could become the pattern.

STATING THE POSITIVES

When your partner makes an effort or does something kind or helpful, seize it as a chance to say something positive – thanks, appreciation or praise. Even if you do not feel warmly deep down, saying it may help you feel less cross. And it will increase the chance that your partner will make the same effort again.

JEALOUSY

This is a common emotion in marriages where there is a drink problem. If the jealousy is in the drinker, it may be an effect of alcohol and jealous ruminations may disappear when the drinking stops. If it does not, then you may need to seek advice. Or, try thinking of it this way. If you fear that someone outside the relationship is threatening it, this probably means that you haven't much confidence in yourself. If you felt confident that you were desirable, capable and strong it would never occur to you to fear that you were losing your lover, unpleasant though that might be. Feelings of inferiority have to be seen for what they are: just fears in your mind. It may be high time that those fears were checked against reality. Start by making a list of your real qualities and all the things you do well (see page 59). Also, recommence doing some of the things you did well in the past. *Make the most of yourself.*

SEX AND YOUR MARRIAGE

On page 12 the effects of alcohol on sex were mentioned. However, frequently it is not just the drinker who is affected, but also the partner. The tension and resentments that may have built up are a powerful dampener on a sexual relationship. In a marriage where the husband being drunk disgusted his wife, she may develop a dislike even of being touched by him. He must try to understand how this came about and approach her with all the more tenderness and patience if at first she cannot respond in the way he would wish.

Bob and Jenny are typical of the many couples who reach their 40s before they really try to have a more fulfilled sexual relationship. One of the chief problems was that Jenny had brought to the marriage attitudes to sex that came from a family where sex was taboo. Because it felt shameful, she had never allowed sex to be thoroughly pleasurable. It took some help from a marriage counsellor until she could accept that she was holding herself back.

Even where the drinking is no longer a problem and the relationship becomes more affectionate, there may still be tension in bed. Perhaps, as in Bob and Jenny's marriage, the difficulties were there before the drinking problem. Here are some suggestions which have helped many couples:

Hints

First, each should help the other to be really relaxed. Atmosphere is important! (People who have used alcohol to relax should know that in larger quantities it interferes with both the male and the female body's ability to respond because of its effect on nerve fibres.) There are no rights or wrongs in sex. What is right is what gives you pleasure and what you can do for your partner that gives him or her pleasure. Tell your partner if there are ways of touching that you find off-putting. Then take it in turns to show each other what you find pleasurable, by guiding the hand for example. Don't overemphasise intercourse. Sex therapists usually ban intercourse until the couple have made new discoveries in touching and caressing, including bringing each other to a climax without intercourse. Only when both partners feel ready should intercourse happen and then only arising out of the initial pleasurable giving and getting. Experienced lovers often devote 20, 30 minutes or longer to exciting and caressing each other before intercourse begins.

Second, never worry about performance. You cannot relax and become sexually aroused if, instead of enjoying the sensations of touching each other, you are worrying about how you are performing. This is the commonest reason for a man to be impotent, i.e. to have difficulty in keeping an erection. Again, an important step in treating impotence is for the sex therapist to ban intercourse while the couple practise touching and caressing for mutual enjoyment. *If a couple stop worrying about intercourse, they can start enjoying sex again.*

Some women who have drinking problems have used alcohol to dull the mind and make sex tolerable because they feel guilty or frightened about sex. If such tension persists despite a loving relationship and tender love-play, then go for help. Kramer and Dunaway's book* is well worth reading. Read it together! But if you have a problem that is persisting why not ask your doctor about it? If the doctor cannot help you, ask to be referred to a specialist, or make enquiries yourself. Family Planning Clinics often provide sex therapy or can redirect you.

WORKING AT MARRIAGE[†]

Any marriage has to be worked at. It cannot be expected simply to run itself. One kind of effort that is needed is the effort it takes to forgive and accept. If your partner makes a blunder, how much pleasanter it is for him or her if the damage is quickly repaired and the long lecture by you is missed out. The same applies to those annoying habits he or she has. If they cannot be changed, don't go on making mountains out of molehills. None of us is perfect. Accept your partner's irritating habits and failings just as you want most of yours accepted. And why not list his or her virtues for a change?

*Why Men Don't Get Enough Sex and Women Don't Get Enough Love, by J. Kramer and D. Dunaway. New York: Pocket Books, 1990, and London: Virgin Books, 1991.

[†]For an unsentimental account of marriage problems and how to tackle them read Making Marriage Work by Paul Hauck, Sheldon Press, 1979.

13

Can friends or colleagues help?

Typically friends, colleagues and supervisors at work try to shield the individual with a drinking problem. For example, they take responsibility for jobs that have not been done, or make excuses to the management. Perhaps they say to themselves, 'I'd drink myself if I had to put up with her mother-in-law/his loneliness/their strain at work.'

Friends, supervisors, employers or colleagues who cover up for the drinker, or ignore the signs, are often harming him or her, not helping. As long as a crisis or confrontation is avoided, the person can continue to drink and harm may result. The crisis which everyone seems so intent on preventing – in the work setting, disciplinary action for example – could actually be a turning point. Sympathy on its own may change nothing, whereas intervening promptly and perhaps pushing the individual into doing something constructive may prevent the problem from worsening.

Having an honest open discussion in these circumstances may not be easy. If the individual is on the defensive, she may try to make you feel a 'drag', a spoil sport: 'Come off it! What's wrong with a drink or two? You're a wet blanket these days!' Or, if you are the employer or manager he may even accuse you of victimising him. You can say, however, that it is not your business to diagnose a drink problem: you want an improvement in your friendship – or an improvement in work performance – and that you want the drinker to seek specialist advice. As an employer you may wish to add, or your company policy may state, that he or she should agree to follow the treatment recommended. At this juncture, obtain the employee's written permission to have progress reports from the specialist or agency where he or she goes for help – not detailed reports with personal information, but sufficient for you to know that the drinker is making a real effort at complying with treatment and facing up to the problem.

Alcohol Concern in London, the Scottish Council on Alcohol, and national and state agencies on alcohol problems in other countries offer advice to companies and organisations on policies related to alcohol problems at work.

If you are a friend, then you will find that much of our advice in Chapter 10 applies to you. You are also welcome to attend Al-Anon meetings (see Appendix).

14

Going for advice

MEDICAL AND PSYCHIATRIC HELP

Your family doctor will understand the problems that arise from excessive drinking and can advise *if you put her fully in the picture.* She will not necessarily send you to a specialist, but may do so if asked, or if she feels it would be helpful. She may prescribe tranquillizers for four or five days if serious withdrawal symptoms are likely, and vitamins. She may suggest you take a deterrent medication for a period.

Psychiatrists are doctors who have had special training in mental illness and also, perhaps, in drinking and drug problems. Psychiatrists seldom ask you to lie on a couch, hypnotise you or give electric shocks. Nor do they have a magic wand. If you are referred to a psychiatrist he may simply offer you and the family doctor some advice. Or he may see you for a series of appointments during which he may go into your background and your present life in order to help you see more clearly what will need to change in order for you to cope more successfully. Don't expect a psychiatrist to hand you a bunch of excuses for your drinking. Perhaps you were unfortunate enough to have had a difficult childhood – but today you are the only one responsible for your drinking.

For many people, stopping drinking or cutting down is the solution to their difficulties. Occasionally after a honeymoon period some of the old personal problems rear their heads again – shyness, feelings of inadequacy, resentments, sexual difficulties. A psychiatrist or psychologist may be able to help at this point. *But there is no miracle cure to any of these problems and the therapist will expect you to work patiently at changing your attitudes and beliefs.*

In the United Kingdom, if you want to see a psychiatrist (either through the NHS or privately) it is usual to ask your family doctor to refer you.

Tests a doctor may do

Drinking affects the liver and the blood cells. Simple blood tests that your general practitioner can do will show the extent of this.

SPECIAL CLINICS

The staff in specialised centres may be doctors, nurses, occupational therapists, psychologists, social workers or specially trained lay people who are sometimes recovered problem drinkers. In general today these clinics do not assume that everyone who comes is an alcoholic who must never drink again. Most clinics include group discussions in their programmes. The group will consist of one or more staff and other patients whose problems are likely to have some element in common with your own. It helps to overcome shame and secrecy if you meet others with whom you can identify. As experiences are shared your own difficulties fall into perspective. You begin to see things as others see them (while drinking you may have had a rather one-sided view of events). Not all groups are just for discussion – for example, instead of theorising about how to refuse drinks when alcohol is being pressed on you, or how to mix well with people at a party if feeling anxious, the group practises doing it. Some clinics build their programmes around the beliefs and principles of Alcoholics Anonymous and offer a spiritual approach as an additional aid to recovery.

Do not be surprised if the clinic wants to contact your family. It is important to have the family's views. Also the clinic may have useful information and advice for them.

All this treatment may be obtained either as an out-patient or as an in-patient. Admission makes the treatment a more intense experience, but is seldom absolutely necessary. People tend to be admitted if withdrawal symptoms are likely to be severe; or if stopping drinking or cutting down has proved impossible while living at home; or if the staff feel there is some important side to your problems that needs closer attention.

Two-thirds of people who go to special clinics are greatly improved a year later.

Can I contact a special clinic myself?

Some centres welcome enquiries and will offer appointments direct; others prefer their clients to be referred by a family doctor.

MEDICATION

Tranquillizers

These can lead to addiction if taken over a long period – they become less effective and the person taking them feels the need to build up the dose. Then withdrawal symptoms begin and a vicious circle is set up, which can lead to alcohol relapse.

Tranquillizers are therefore best used only for a few days at a time, for example in the four or five days after stopping very heavy drinking. Sleeping tablets should also only be used for very short periods, if at all (see pages 35 and 63).

In the 1990s some non-addictive drugs may become available that could help to reduce relapse in the first months of recovery. They will only be an aid to abstinence, not a cure. They will not end the need to work at changing attitudes, and to find ways of reacting to problems and arranging an alcohol-free lifestyle.

Anti-depressants

Some people who are depressed, usually those whose depression is severe and fits the medical syndrome of 'depressive illness', benefit from these drugs. They correct chemical imbalances in the parts of the brain that control mood, not by supplying an instant euphoriant but by preserving healthy levels of the brain's own chemicals.

Anti-depressants are not addictive and are safe, but side-effects are common in the first few days. These vary according to the type of drug and include dry mouth, drowsiness or nausea. It is important to persevere through the side-effect period, and give it at least three weeks before deciding whether or not you are benefiting. Anti-depressants work very gradually, and only lift depression and relieve accompanying fears and anxiety over a period of several weeks, not in a few days.

Deterrent medication

'Antabuse' and 'Abstem' ('Dipsan', and in Canada 'Temposil') are substances which if taken regularly in the correct dose cause an unpleasant, even dangerous, reaction if alcohol enters the body (flushing, headache, nausea, pounding feelings or faintness). If the aim is to stop drinking completely, these pills are a useful insurance policy. Once you are taking these pills you know that you must not drink for at least five days – or seven in the case of Antabuse.

Helen's husband was a busy company director, a reserved man at the best of times, and she often felt he ignored her, even belittled her. A pattern of drinking developed whereby she was often drunk when he arrived home. She knew she was driving him further away; she felt disgusted with herself. Yet only two or three weeks later she would once more find herself feeling hurt about something, buy a bottle of sherry and escape into semi-consciousness again. As tension mounted in the marriage she felt more and more depressed, until during one drinking session she tried to kill herself. At that point, realising that she could not expect her husband to change overnight into someone always warm and caring, she decided to take a deterrent tablet. She wrote to us: 'Taking the tablet was the most tremendous help. Having to be without the crutch of alcohol meant I was able gradually to build up confidence in myself and come to realise that I could do everything I wanted to and do it well.' She found a part-time job and this time kept it, took a class at college and worked at being more independent and confident.

For the person who *wants* to abstain, these medicines help establish a period of stability in which to get life reorganised. Injured self-esteem has a chance to recover. Determination has time to become established. It gives a chance to find out that life without alcohol is possible.

Is it weakness to rely on a pill instead of willpower?

The trouble with willpower is that it is not always at its best when you need it. With these pills a decision to drink or not to drink still has to be made, but only once a day.

Is there anything I should avoid?

When taking these pills avoid food that contains alcohol, such as trifle; large quantities of vinegar made from wine or cider or pickles using such vinegar; cough medicines and mouth rinses containing alcohol.

Alcohol-containing products for the skin or eau de cologne can very occasionally cause a skin reaction: test a small amount. Most medicines, including antibiotics and pain-killers, can be used as normal, but if you are having a tooth extraction tell your dentist so that he uses an alcohol-free anaesthetic.

If you are out with friends who might spike your drink, keep your eye on it.

Occasionally people want to stay on alcohol-deterrent tablets for years. However, they are medicines and should only be taken with medical advice.

Should I ask someone to check I take it?

The deterrent method only works for as long as you take the tablet regularly. If you are likely to start missing it, perhaps because deep down you want to drink, ask your partner or someone at work to check you are taking it. Put the tablet into water, so that it breaks up, and then you cannot hide it under your tongue and pretend you have swallowed it. Your supervisor can also check that you have not substituted aspirins, because Antabuse and Abstem tablets are marked.

Vitamins

Heavy drinkers often run short of their body stores of vitamins, especially the B vitamins. Vitamins can be bought over the counter of a chemist's or obtained on prescription. Some studies find that heavy drinkers have low levels of zinc in their bodies. Zinc supplement tablets can also be bought from the pharmacist.

ALCOHOLICS ANONYMOUS

Much of the present-day concern and sympathy for the problem drinker is due to AA, whose members for 50 years have shown the world that a man or woman can have a severe drink problem but may want to recover and can achieve this. AA has grown spectacularly in the past 20 years. It exists only to help individuals overcome the problem. There are no membership fees. The only requirement for AA membership is a desire to stop drinking. At an AA meeting there is a warm informal welcome for newcomers – it is a fellowship in which all have in common the fact that their drinking at one time or another caused harm. During the meeting, members talk about their own experiences. Newcomers learn that others have had similar experiences with alcohol. They learn that they are not alone. Most importantly, they learn that recovery is possible.

'What's the point,' some people say, 'of going over your own story again and again?' Paul explained as follows: 'To remember just how bad my life was when I was drinking is important to me today. I was a very sick person when I finally reached out for help. I had lost the will to go on living. I was utterly beaten. I don't want to forget where I came from. If at a meeting I can pass on the tiny ray of hope that was given to me and changed my life three years ago then I am truly grateful for the opportunity to be able to do so.'

AA members have not found it possible to drink again with any certainty that it will be safe. They recommend abstinence. They know the relief that comes when problem drinkers cease to struggle to control their drinking, admit they have lost the fight and surrender to the realisation that they are 'powerless over alcohol'.

Some AA writing and speaking is spiritual. People whose lives have been transformed since starting to go to AA feel that there must have been a guiding force helping them to achieve what they have achieved. Who knows? It is possible. But do not be put off if you are not a religious person and a member mentions God. Just as with any approach, take out of it what you need. There is wisdom stored up in the customs and sayings of AA, and a vast understanding of people who drink. Give yourself three or four meetings to allow you time to begin to see how it works. In most areas there is more than one meeting – try several.

How can I contact AA?

Look in your local newspaper, phone directory or directory enquiries under Alcoholics Anonymous. Your Citizen's Advice Bureau may also give a number to call or tell you the time and place of a meeting in your area (see Appendix).

AL-ANON AND AL-ATEEN

Like AA, Al-Anon groups can be found in most cities and large towns in Britain. The members are husbands, wives, parents, children and friends of people with drinking problems. They offer advice and support.

Al-Anon is not the place for people to moan about what terrible partners they have. People are there to talk about where they may have gone wrong without being made to feel guilty, and to work out how they can take a more effective attitude to their problems. The approach is warm, welcoming and above all understanding. Go to several meetings before deciding whether or not their approach will be useful to you.

Al-Ateen is for the teenage children of drinkers.

How can I contact them?

Via Alcoholics Anonymous, or see Appendix.

COUNCILS ON ALCOHOL AND ADVICE CENTRES

Councils on Alcohol and Alcohol Advice Centres are voluntary bodies, usually with one or two paid staff. They offer advice, information and sometimes counselling. No charge is made to clients, though donations are accepted. They have strict rules about confidentiality. There is sometimes an informal social side to their activities, which is helpful to the person who is having difficulty making new friends or finding ways of spending spare time.

How can I contact them?

Phone for an appointment or just go along. Check the local phone book or newspaper or obtain the address of your nearest Council from the National Office (see Appendix).

RESIDENTIAL HELP/HOSTELS

Isolation is common among problem drinkers who have lost touch with family and friends. Many cities have living-in facilities for such people, if they are in the process of trying to find a new lifestyle. These are run by social work departments, voluntary organisations or one of the churches. Skilled help is available, but residents are expected to take an active part in the running of the hostel. Abstinence is usually the goal of residents. Although you may have your own room, the emphasis is on living as a member of a group. These facilities are not to be confused with lodging houses or shelters for the homeless.

How can I contact them?

Through your local social work department or Council on Alcohol (see Appendix).

OTHER ORGANISATIONS

See Appendix.

15

Surely it's not that easy?

For many people, once they have made a decision to do something about their drinking, it is easy. Others may have a number of false starts. For them it becomes a matter of experimenting to find the best strategy – but scientific experimentation requires an honest objective unbiased observer, so if you are having repeated experiments you should seek help from an outsider.

If trying to become a normal drinker is not working out, you should have a period of several months completely free of alcohol.

If you have set out to abstain but find you keep 'breaking out', EITHER:

- Plan an attempt at normal drinking, closely following the guide on page 41 and with a third party to give you honest advice about it; OR
- Contact AA; or request a deterrent drug for a period from your doctor; or get an appointment at a special centre.

Ian (see page 30), who chose abstinence as his best solution, put it like this: 'I assure you it's not all fight. In fact, I must say that it was easier than I imagined. At the beginning, one reason why I had not wanted to admit my problem was that I imagined giving up would be so difficult. I am not saying stopping drinking was easy, but with an understanding wife, some professional help and a wish to succeed, it was easier than I had feared ... Now I see that the fact that I drank, that I felt I needed it and could not do without it, was a state of mind. Now I've changed my way of thinking. I've reprogrammed myself.'

Never give up trying to find your solution. The odds are in your favour.

Agencies offering help

Councils on Alcohol and Alcohol Advice Agencies
To be found throughout the UK. The address of the council or agency in your area can be obtained from your telephone directory, or from one of the following:

Alcohol Concern
275 Gray's Inn Road
London WC1X 8QF
071-833 3471

Scottish Council on Alcohol
147 Blythswood Street
Glasgow G2 4EN
041-333 9677

Alcoholics Anonymous
There are hundreds of AA meetings worldwide, in towns, cities and rural areas. For information on times and locations of meetings near you, look up AA in your phone directory or contact:
Great Britain except London: 0904 644 026
Greater London: 071 352 3001
Northern Ireland: 0232 681 084
Scotland: 041 221 9027
For literature, and world contact numbers: **UK General Services Office**
PO Box 1
Stonebow House
Stonebow
York YO1 2NJ
0904 644026

Al-Anon Family Groups
61 Great Dover Street
London SE1 4YF
071-403 0888

IRELAND

AA
Dublin Service Office
109 S. Circular Road
Leonard's Corner
Dublin 8
0001 538 998

Irish Council on Alcohol
19/20 Fleet Street
Dublin 2
0001 774 649

CANADA

Addresses of agencies in each province can be obtained from:

Health Services and Promotion Branch
Jeanne Mance Building
Tunney's Pasture
Ottawa
Ontario K1A 1B4
613-957 7800

Alcoholics Anonymous
Toronto Intergroup
234 Eglinton Avenue East
Toronto
Ontario M4P 1K5
416-487 5591

AUSTRALIA

AA
General Service Office
PO Box 25
Beaconsfield
NSW 2014
02 663 1206

Alcohol and Drug Foundation Australia
19-33 Townshend Street
Philip
ACT 2606
62 810686

NEW ZEALAND

AA
PO Box 6458
Wellington
04 859 455

Al-Anon
Suite 4
Charter House
56 Customs Street
Auckland
09 794 871

Alcohol Liquor Advisory Council
National Insurance House
119–123 Featherstone Street
PO Box 5023
Wellington
44 720997

USA

AA World Services
PO Box 459
Grand Central Station
New York
NY 10163
212 686 1100

Further reading

Alcoholics Anonymous. The 'Big Book' of AA, written by its 100 founders, obtainable from AA addresses above.

Twelve Steps and Twelve Traditions. How members of AA recover and how the fellowship functions.

Of Course You're Angry: a Guide to Dealing with the Emotions of Chemical Dependence, by G. Rosellini and M. Worden. Center City, Minn., USA: Hazelden Press, 19XX.

Addictive Thinking: Why Do We Lie to Ourselves? Why Do Others Believe Us?, by A.J. Twerski. Center City, Minn., USA: Hazelden Press, 1990.

Healing the Addictive Mind, by L. Jampolsky. Berkeley, Ca., USA: Celestial Arts 1991.

Beating the Blues: a Self-help Approach to Overcoming Depression, by S. Tanner and J. Ball. London: Sheldon Press, and Melbourne, Australia: Doubleday Books, 1989.

Your Erroneous Zones, by W. Dyer. London: Sphere Books, 1976. Still in print; a great read about getting over anxiety, low self-esteem and self-destructive thinking and behaviour.

Feel the Fear and Do It Anyway: How to Turn your Fear and Indecision into Confidence and Action, by S. Jeffers, London: Arrow Books, 1987.

MARRIAGE

How to Stay Married: a Practical and Inspiring Do-it-yourself Guide, by C. Lane and L. Stevens. London: Arrow Books, 1987.

Why Men Don't Get Enough Sex and Women Don't Get Enough Love, by J. Kramer and D. Dunaway. New York: Pocket Books, 1990, and London: Virgin Books 1991.

FOR THE FAMILY

If You Really Loved Me: How to Survive any Addiction in the Family, by J. and J. Ditzler, London: Papermac, 1989.

Codependency: How to Break Free and Live Your Own Life, by D. Stafford and L. Hodgkinson. London: Piatkus, 1991.

Index